JAKE DELLAHUNT, VINEYARD LAWYER
(with an office on the Cape)
A.J. Cushner

Martin Sisters Publishing

Published by

Ivy House Books, a division of Martin Sisters Publishing, LLC

www.martinsisterspublishing.com

Copyright © 2012 by A.J. Cushner

ISBN: 978-1-937273-42-2
Mystery
Editor: Kathleen Papajohn

Printed in the United States of America
Martin Sisters Publishing, LLC

For The Putchkie Boy — Ben and his big brothers,
Max and Liam McCarthy

An imprint of Martin Sisters Publishing, LLC

FOREWORD AND ACKNOWLEDGEMENT

One of the few benefits of growing old lies in the treasured memories of places and people we revisit that seemed ordinary at the time, but in retrospect were quite spectacular. Martha's Vineyard was one of those magical places along with the cast of characters who lived there. Long before the Vineyard became a popular celebrity resort, if you saw more than a dozen people on a white pristine beach, it was a happening. Status wasn't measured in wealth, but on how many years you could manage to keep your old island car running and how many places would cash a personal check. In the mornings, dogs ran wild with excitement chasing sticks thrown into the surf and nights were filled with trips to the Carousel in Oak Bluffs.

The years passed, but I find myself caught up in the island's legendary beauty where once I drove along tree-shaded roads, past up-island meadows and sleepy farms that fell into the sea. There was a time when I sat alone on the deck of a night ferry and watched the mainland fade away. The exquisite natural sanctuary offered me peace for so many years, it was always on my mind to write about some of the people and events that happened - or almost happened.

The book was conceived by reading and listening to years of island yarns and myths and then put to the pen. As much as some would like to believe otherwise, Jake Dellahunt and the characters in these stories are not real people. They are bits and pieces of people living only in my imagination.

Like so many things in life, a novel is a collaborative effort. On-island with my brother and sister-in-law, Dick and Estelle Cushner, the idea for the novel about a dysfunctional island lawyer and his quirky cases and friends percolated and took root. Graciously nourished and encouraged by my wife Myrna Cushner, and with the support of friends and family, I was able to complete the manuscript in a little over one year. Editors, Freda Spencer, Marian O'Brien Paul and Joanne Greenburg made much of my writing clearer and the reading better. Thanks go to Barbara Gentile Bennet-White of Brookline, Massachusetts for reviewing the manuscript and Gilbert Meyers of Boynton Beach, for his help and valued suggestions. Thanks also go to photographer Ernest C. White of East Dennis, Massachusetts for the photo on the back cover. They have all given unselfishly of their time and talent. Thank you my friends and God bless all of you.

A. J. Cushner
May 30, 2012

Chapter One

The Case of the Wild Indians

After Jake Dellahunt lost the family he loved, he left the city and never looked back. It had been five years since he collected his diplomas from the walls of a high-rise office in downtown Boston and "temporarily" hung them in a second floor walk-up above Grapes of Wrath Bookstore on Martha's Vineyard. There were better places on the island to rent, but the owner of the bookstore sealed the deal with a promise of a brass sign and a fifty percent discount off any new book Jake wanted. The brass sign at the bottom of the stairs read, "Jacoby Dellahunt, Attorney at Law, Office Hours 9:00 a.m. to 4:00 p.m., Weekdays – One Flight Up."

Jake had moved into the Mathews Cottage on the shore of Lake Tashmoo, across the dirt road that cut through a sea of beach grass and then snaked its way along a tangle of beach plums and stunted salt water pines.

Judge Samuel Mathews had never married and when he died, Jake Dellahunt inherited the house on Martha's Vineyard from his old law partner. The weathered, shingled cottage with its pitched peaked roof, floor to ceiling windows and broad wooden decks was peacefully nestled on a knoll above a salt water estuary. Jake liked the spot because it was hidden from storms and the IRS.

It was an early island-morning and a bank of fog covered the edges of the pond like a blanket of late winter snow. Not far from the edge of the water, a large Wampanoag Indian sat cross-legged under an old wooden sailboat that was supported by two sagging wooden horses. When he saw Jake Dellahunt coming down the path, he carefully placed the paintbrush he held in his hand on top of a paint can and looked up.

Jake held out a thermos of hot coffee. "I brought you something for your break, Chief."

"Almost finished with the bottom. Another few days and you will be able to sail to the shores of our new Wampanoag Tribal Lands," the big Indian said, referring to the lawsuit the Tribal Council had filed against the government. The Tribal Council had approached Jake twice, asking him to take a federal case to restore their rights to lands in Gay Head and he turned them down twice. "However you, Jake Dellahunt," the large Indian continued, "shall need a special visa to enter into the sacred lands of our Tribal Nation."

Jake smiled and dismissed the gentle political jibe. He knew the Indians would probably never forgive him for refusing to represent them. "I've got my passport ready just in case the final score is Indians, 1 and White Man, 0," he said and passed the thermos to the Indian. Then he ran his hand over the painted wooden planks and the wet caulking compound.

"Careful, it's still wet," the Wampanoag Indian warned and took a swig out of the thermos. "Oh hell, it's coffee."

Jake laughed. At one time, Robert Paul was Chief of the Tribal Council. He had worked for Judge Sam while he was alive and for Jake for nearly ten years. There wasn't much the two men didn't know about each other. Jake fished a small silver flask from his shirt pocket. "You missed a few spots, Chief." He unscrewed the cap and poured the shot into the thermos. "This might improve your caulking job some."

"Have not finished. You go back to whatever you were *not* doing and I will finish here. Then I will start on the power boat and the traps in the shed."

"That can wait. It's May, and the boys won't be here for another month."

"Mmmm. Many moons have passed since they have fished these waters," Robert Paul said and laughed at his version of a Hollywood Indian.

Jake was not amused. "Nearly five years. I wonder what they think of a father who hasn't laid eyes on them for five years."

"The boys love you with their hearts, boss, not with their eyes."

"Chief, they love you more than me. You didn't hurt them. You were the one who took them fishing and taught them the ways of the island. Not me."

"This is a chance to put all those demons behind you."

Just then, Jake's cell phone rang. He pulled it out of his pocket and looked at the calling number. An island number he did not recognize. He hit the green button.

"Mr. Dellahunt?"

"Yes."

"This is your neighbor at the end of the road. Ya know, Manny Campos, the long-line swordfish captain."

"Yes, Captain Manny. I haven't seen you around lately. How are you?"

"Not too good. Guess I may have done somethin' real dumb."

"How's that?"

"I need a lawyer. I think I shot my wife last night."

*

Jake had to put off interviewing Captain Manny until they finished processing him at the county jail in Edgartown. He decided to have an early lunch in Vineyard Haven and pulled his 1992 Ford F-150 4x4 pickup into the parking lot in back of Frank's

Island Café and Donut Shop. Frank Falcone, the donut shop owner was hauling forty pound bags from the bed of an old pickup truck and two employees were piling them inside a storage shed behind the café and donut shop.

Jake stopped and watched them for a minute. He thought it odd for Frank to be making his own deliveries. "What you got there, Frank? Cement bags? Trying to make your donuts heavier, if that's at all possible."

"Very funny, smart guy. No, it's sugar. Price of sugar's gone through the roof. Just storing it for now, but we use a crap load of sugar making donuts in season. How about some help?"

Jake looked at the painfully large bags and shook his head. "No thank you, Frank. I went to law school because there was a sign on the front door that read, "Boston University School of Law, No Heavy Lifting Required.""

After lunch, Jake made a quick stop to check on Captain Manny's wife in Oak Bluffs at the All-Island Vineyard Hospital and then headed down the Shore Road to speak to Manny Campos, the sword fisherman. On the way to the Dukes County House of Correction in Edgartown, Jake got to thinking about the Indian land claims and his decision to turn down the case. It wasn't easy. Robert Paul, his best friend and handyman had asked him to take their case. He refused. He thought it was a career-ending law case. If he lost the land claims, hundreds of Native Americans in Gay Head and on Cape Cod would forever hold him responsible. If he won, Jake thought hundreds of homeowners in Gay Head would lose their property without being compensated, which would undoubtedly alienate most of the homeowners on the island. Either way, he believed the case was suicide for an island lawyer.

In his heart of hearts, Jake believed no court would overturn three hundred years of property ownership. The Wampanoag were certain to lose. Still, he thought the Indians had cleared some preliminary hurdles that normally trip up most Indian land claims. They had produced the original land grants King George issued the

Wampanoag with defined borders reaching from Lighthouse Road in the North down to Moshup Trail in the South, some twelve square miles of exquisite views of cliffs and hills falling into the sea. It was also an area where hundreds of people owned very expensive summer homes. The Indian Tribe was only waiting for the Department of Indian Affairs to certify them as a Native American Tribe and declare the current members of the Tribe had sufficient bloodlines tied to their ancestors to grant them standing to make claims.

*

Jake parked his pick-up outside a large, white colonial house in Edgartown, which was indistinguishable from dozens of other large, white, colonial clapboard houses on Main Street in Edgartown - except this white colonial was the county lockup. As was his practice when he interviewed clients in jail, Jake had called ahead. He sat waiting at one end of a table in the small windowless conference room located on the first floor. After a few minutes, Jake's client walked in dressed in the standard orange Dukes County jailhouse coveralls. The Deputy closed the door and Jake stood up and motioned the swordfish boat captain to sit across the table from him.

Before sitting down, Manny Campos bent over and whispered most peculiarly, "Did I really kill her, Mr. Dellahunt? I mean, did I? Is she dead?"

Jake thought it was an astonishingly bizarre question. It didn't make much sense to him. He waited until the client was seated before answering. He opened his briefcase and took out a legal pad. "You don't have to whisper. We're alone here. No, Manny. She's in ICU, the intensive care unit at the Vineyard Hospital."

Jake looked up from his notepad. He was surprised at the size of the man sitting opposite him. Campos was so tall he could hardly fit his knees under the table. He had seen Manny Campos many times, but always inside of an old blue pick-up truck the fisherman drove along Cottage Road. Jake judged he was a man in his early fifties, square faced, broad shouldered, with graying beard and salt and pepper hair. Manny owned the property at the end of the road and lived quietly in a modest cabin with his wife and twelve year-old daughter.

Jake thought Campos looked drained and pale. Maybe it was the night in the lockup, maybe something else. "Can you start from the beginning and tell me what happened last night?"

Campos sat stoically looking at Jake without saying a word. It seemed to take a moment for Jake's question to sink in. "My people was on this tiny strip of land a long time, Mr. Dellahunt. My family's come here from the Azores more 'n hundred and fifty years ago to work the whaling ships out of New Bedford and Edgartown. When people didn't need no more whale oil to light their lamps, we took to boats and fished. We're Portuguese. Fishing's our life. The ocean, she's in our blood. I went out to sea with my father when I was fourteen. And now, well now looks like I'll be the last of the Campos fisherman."

"Can you tell me what happened last night?"

Campos sat stone-faced and paid no attention to Jake's question and just rambled on. "When you go to the market to buy a piece of fish for dinner, do you really think you're just buying fish? Do you know what you're buying, Mr. Dellahunt? You're not just paying for a piece of fish. You're buying pieces of men's lives. What price you pay for fish is cheap. What we pay is the real price. The sea, she took my grandfather and then she swallowed up my father."

Campos turned and looked directly at Jake. "The sea is a beautiful woman. She smiles and beckons you to come to her. She will take you and bring you to her breast and kiss you. For a while, she will let you have your way with her. She will let you think you are her master and, when you come to love and finally trust her, that's the day she will drain the last breath from your body. That's the moment she will possess you. And when she is finished with you, her sharks and crabs will pick the skin off your bones. They'll pull the eyes out of your sockets and leave your brains shredded 'till you're no more 'n a bleached white skeleton rolling around her muddy bottom."

Jake heard and saw the momentary madness in Manny's eyes. At first, Jake didn't understand Manny's answer. Maybe Manny was trying to tell him what had happened in some strange way. Jake thought Manny seemed to say he had been seduced by a woman, someone who had taken over his life and she was the sea.

As the fisherman continued, his voice grew louder and more strained. "Every time I go out, I ask myself why, why do I play dice with my life? Sooner or later I know it comes out snake-eyes. I know this. But then I see her. I want to be with her again. She is so beautiful. I cannot help myself."

Jake looked at Manny's twisted mouth and salty eyes. "I want to know what happened," Jake insisted. "Tell me, what happened last night."

Campos said nothing. He shook his head.

"I can't help you Mr. Campos unless you tell me what happened last night."

"It would be more 'n last night. We was three weeks at sea, loaded with five thousand pounds of swordfish on ice. We lay heavy in the water, was more 'n a hundred miles out off the banks when the storms come up, one right after 'n other. Four days of hell she showed us. Never seen it so bad. Black skies and blinding rain so thick she turned day to night. Waves as tall as container ships. Winds took our life raft, blew away our deck rigging and knocked us down twice. Do you know what that means? The boat rolled over on its side. Two men went into the water and disappeared. She took them fast. Men with wives and children. I couldn't do nothin' to save them.

"After she flooded the boat, the power went dead. We had no batteries, no engine, 'n no radio. She crushed us broadside with mountains of her waves. She looked us straight in the face and split us in half. We were in survival gear when she took the boat. The four of us which was left jumped into her arms. Three hours we waited for help in freezing water. After a while, a Coast Guard chopper came and pulled up three; never found the others. When I got home last night, when I got home last night," he repeated and went no further. There were tears in his eyes.

"What happened?"

"I can't remember a damned thing."

As much as he tried, after he walked into the house that night, Manny Campos had no memory of what happened.

*

Robert Paul set down two plates of steaming hot sea bass fish stew on the supper table and then pulled up a chair. "I asked the Tribe to hire you for the Settlement Conference, boss. I hope you're not going to refuse us this time."

Jake poured a second slug of Dewar's into the glass sitting on the table and looked at the plate of food in front of him. "I must be missing something here, Chief. What's this Settlement Conference all about?"

The big Indian sat down, picked up a fork and began eating.

"Start eating while it's hot, boss. It's fresh sea bass. Trapped it this morning."

"I'll get to the fish in a minute. Has the court ordered the Tribe to a Settlement Conference?"

"Didn't you hear?"

"I've been on the phone to Boston, talking about dissociative mental disorders with Mickey Rosenbaum most of the afternoon."

"Do you mean Dr. Rosenbaum, the Harvard shrink guy, who shows up on the island one day a week? If you're paying good money to him to stop your drinking, why are you hitting the bottle tonight? Why would you throw away your money on that quack? Little Franny Meezum can whip the spirits out of you for next to nothing. You'll never touch another drop of whiskey again when he finishes with you."

Jake set his glass down. "Wait a minute. Are you talking about that weirdo, Little Franny, who lives with six barking dogs in a teepee next to the light house?"

"He's no weirdo, Jake. He's a bony-fied, certified, licensed tribal medicine man. Franny Meezum knows more medicine than in all Doc Rosenbaum's books. And his dogs are souls who have passed into the spirit world."

"Then why are they always barking and snarling at him?"

"They are the spirits of his ex-wives," Robert Paul answered quickly. "You know Jake, we're not all just a bunch of wild Indians. Why does the White Man find it so easy to believe all Indians are stupid and superstitious? When Franny was a child, the Tribal Council sent him to school off-island. He got some real school learning. He can stop you from drinking, alright."

Jake laughed at the thought of being treated by an Indian medicine man. "First, Dr. Rosenbaum isn't treating me. I called Rosenbaum to talk to him about Manny Campos. And second, having one or two shots before dinner isn't 'hitting the bottle again.'" Jake put the bottle of Dewar's back in the cabinet, spilled the rest of the glass into the sink and then poured a cup of coffee. He swallowed a mouthful. "There, feel better now, Chief?"

"Sit down and eat," the Indian chided Jake. "You know I saw a car go down the road toward Captain Manny's house many nights. And it come back in the early morning. Same car. You think something funny's going on while Captain Manny go out fishing?"

"Maybe. They've been married a long time and I never heard anything like that about her. What about you?"

Robert Paul shook his head. "No, nothing. But I remember my third wife would wait until the moon was full and the village was asleep before she run off and howl at the moon like a wolf. Nobody knew about her either."

Robert Paul waited for the right moment. "You know boss, there were some suits pokin' their nose around the Cottage Road today. I think they may be lookin' for you."

"Ah, it's May, isn't it? It's time for our two-legged friends from Infernal Revenue to make their rounds on Martha's Vineyard. They come over to the island once or twice a year and try to collect from everyone who owes. That's just about everyone who lives here. Cheezus, they'd chase you to Timbuktu to collect a dime. And don't be letting them in the house without a warrant, which no judge on this island will ever give them."

"Why don't you just pay them?"

"I do, but evidently not fast enough."

The two men sat silently locked in their thoughts. Finally Robert Paul said, "Well, are you going represent us in the Settlement Conference or not? They will want to know."

Jake ate silently and thought about it. When he finished dinner, he picked up his plate and headed for the sink. "You know what this means, don't you?"

"No."

"It means if the Tribal Council refuses to settle the claim at the Settlement Conference, the court is going to appoint a Special Federal Commission. They'll establish the value of the land, get Congress to make some kind of token restitution payment for a fraction of the current value and then award the Tribe a small parcel of land nobody wants. That's what they did on Cape Cod, in Rhode Island and New Hampshire."

"They can't do that, boss."

"They're the government. They can do whatever they want."

"But we got laws."

"Yes, and the White Man makes them. You want me to go to the bargaining table for you. Fine, I'll go, but the Tribe has to understand what's coming down. If they don't accept the government's settlement offer, then the court will order a federal commission to ram a deal down their throat. They can appeal, but you're certain to lose under the Federal Native American Land Settlement Act. The federal commission has the plenary power to come up with an amount and that's it, unless you can show fraud or some illegal mischief, like a pervasive bias against Indians.

"Bias against Indians? That should not be hard to prove."

"You would think, wouldn't you?"

The Indian nodded his head and grunted, indicating he understood Jake.

"You still sure you want me to represent the Tribe."

"We trust you, boss. Not the Boston lawyers."

"Remember, Chief, I was once a Boston lawyer."

*

Jake knew how to work the legal system. Manny's case was scheduled for a preliminary Probable Cause Hearing in the District Court. Jake loved Probable Cause Hearings where he could put his witnesses on the stand to testify and he could cross-examine the DA's witnesses. If he convinced the judge there was insufficient probable cause to hold Manny, the case was over. But if the DA convinced the District Court Judge there was sufficient cause, the case would be sent to the Grand Jury and then to Superior Court for trial.

Jake liked the quirky procedure because it gave Manny Campos two bites at the same apple. Jake mostly liked Probable Cause Hearings in the District Court because he played poker with the District Court Judge on Thursday nights. But then again, so did Alice Wishansky, the Major Felony Prosecutor for the county.

Jake drove to the painted, red brick District Court on Main Street in Edgartown. It hadn't changed much in more than 160 years. He could see Chappaquiddick Island, just across the harbor from Edgartown. He had his first glimpse of the little red courthouse in 1969 when Senator "Ted" Kennedy went on TV and pleaded guilty to reduced charges in connection with the drowning of Mary Jo Kopechne.

Word of the shooting on Cottage Road traveled quickly. Jake saw the three meager rows of wooden spectator benches behind the heavily varnished wooden railing in the small courtroom had filled quickly for the Wednesday morning arraignments. At the defense table, Jake sat between his client and his paralegal, Penny Pacheco. Fifteen feet to Jake's right, the Dukes County District Attorney, Al Norton, with ruddy face and hands, overweight and dressed in a grey flannel suit with matching vest sat next to his Major Felony Prosecutor, Alice Wishansky. A half dozen island lawyers sat in the chairs behind Jake waiting for their cases to be called.

Jake glanced over at Alice. She was ten years younger than him, horned rimmed glasses, snarly dark hair, not unattractive, never in makeup, dressed in a blue skirt and jacket and very smart. She smiled her patented Cheshire cat grin, one that reminded him of last Thursday night's poker game when she held a hand with a straight flush. Jake was aware she was cunning at cards and the most dangerous in a courtroom when she was smiling. Jake turned and nodded to her when the Judge entered and stood before the bench.

The clerk called out, *"All Stand. Hear ye, hear ye, hear ye. All persons having anything to do before the Dukes County District Court, Justices of the District Court, draw near and give your attention and you shall be heard, Justice James J. McNaught presiding. God save the Commonwealth of Massachusetts and this honorable court. You may be seated."*

Judge McNaught, a short man, with a sober look about him, took his seat. He quickly disposed of two matters at bench conferences with the lawyers who had been seated behind Jake and opened the docket for the Manny Campos attempted murder case. No matter how many times Jake had faced this moment, he felt his heart skip to his throat when the case was called. *"Docket Number 12-1851, Commonwealth of Massachusetts vs. Manuel J. Campos.*

Both Jake and Alice Wishansky stood up.

Jake quickly said, "If it please the court, Defendant waives the reading of the Complaint."

Judge McNaught had a no-nonsense reputation for being quick-on-the-draw when it came to making his decisions. Once he got an idea in his head, there was no shaking it loose. He adjusted his silver metal-rimmed glasses with his boney fingers and scanned the Complaint. When he finished, he removed them and looked at Manny. His eyes narrowed. It was clear Judge McNaught did not like what he had just read in the charge. He looked straight at Manny and asked, "How do you wish to plead, Mr. Campos?"

Manny looked as if he had just arrived from another planet and said nothing.

"Does your client understand the question, Mr. Dellahunt?"

Jake answered for him. "Defendant stands mute to the Complaint."

Judge McNaught responded, "I'll enter a 'not guilty' plea, for you, Mr. Campos. Is there any reason, your client doesn't want to answer the Complaint at this time, Mr. Dellahunt?"

"Thank you, Judge," Jake said respectfully, being careful not to antagonize him. "As to answering the Complaint at this time, he can't. He seems to have suffered a mental breakdown. He's incompetent to make a plea, answer the Complaint, and assist in his defense to stand trial. He's plainly incompetent to stand trial."

Alice Wishansky jumped up. "Plainly incompetent? He was competent enough to empty a revolver at his wife. She's on a hospital respirator fighting for her life. He shot her in front of his twelve year-old daughter while he was screaming the worst obscenities at the poor woman."

The judge banged his gavel and derisively said, "Thank you, Ms. Wishansky for that carefully crafted legal argument. I hope you feel better getting that out of your craw."

The spectators laughed and the Judge looked at them sternly and returned to Alice. "Now sit down and let's get on with the arraignment."

Alice paid no attention. "Your Honor, Mr. Dellahunt is trying to set up an incompetency defense. I believe I have the right to be heard on any issues of legal competency or insanity defenses."

Judge McNaught banged his gavel once again and said, "Sit down Alice or I'm going to fine you for contempt. Let's hear what Jake has to say about the defendant's incompetency. I'll hear from you both on a twenty day psychiatric evaluation order at Bridgewater State Hospital."

Alice sat down and the judge turned to Jake. "Do you wish a court ordered psychiatric evaluation at Bridgewater?"

"I don't think that will be necessary, Judge. Dr. Michael Rosenbaum is a highly respected Mass General Hospital psychiatrist, who sees patients on Martha's Vineyard on Thursdays. He will be here for his regular visit tomorrow and I have asked Dr. Rosenbaum to examine Mr. Campos and be ready to give the Court his findings. He has assured me he will be able to give us his findings on Friday if the court wants to dispose of this matter quickly."

Judge McNaught opened his desk diary and looked at his calendar. "I see I am scheduled to be at a Judges' conference in Atlanta for two weeks beginning Monday."

The judge turned to Alice. "Would the Commonwealth prefer to wait until I return from Atlanta?"

Alice stood up and smiled her most alluring Cheshire grin Jake had ever seen blanket her face. "No, the Commonwealth does not need more time. We will be ready for a Friday competency hearing."

"Now you both understand it's the day after tomorrow. There will be no continuances granted."

Jake and Alice nodded.

"Ms. Wishansky, is Dr. Rosenbaum acceptable to you as a defense expert or does the Commonwealth have an objection at this time?"

Alice rose to her feet. "I know Dr. Rosenbaum by reputation. I am willing to accept Dr. Rosenbaum as an expert for the defense on the issue of competency if Your Honor will permit Dr. Charles

Cross, a psychologist who has a summer house on the island to examine the defendant on behalf of the government."

"Any objection, Mr. Dellahunt?"

"A moment, Your Honor."

"You have thirty seconds," the Judge responded.

Alice smiled and Jake did not like "the tell" of the hand she was playing. He turned and whispered to his paralegal, Penny, "Do you know this psychologist, Charles Cross?"

"I've seen his name. I believe he's got a place in Chilmark," she whispered back.

Jake quietly said to her, "He's not a psychiatrist with an MD degree. I'm sure he hasn't the credentials or the weight Mickey Rosenbaum is going to bring into court."

"Do you want me to Google him in the clerk's office?"

Jake thought about it a moment. "He's probably here doing some spring cleaning and asked Alice to be put on her expert witness list. Anyways, we always have a chance to challenge him at the probable cause hearing and later if it goes to the Superior Court." It was a no brainer for Jake. He stood up and declared, "Defense has no objection."

The judge banged down his gavel. "Then we stand adjourned until Friday at 10:00 AM."

*

The rest of the day passed quickly. Early the next morning, Jake walked along Main Street in Vineyard Haven thinking about the poker game that night. Talking law cases was absolutely off limits at the Thursday night weekly card game, but he knew Alice Wishansky just might make the fatal mistake of trying to score points with Judge McNaught. He thought the opportunity would prove to be irresistible for her. If she did, Jake was convinced McNaught wouldn't forgive nor forget.

Jake turned the corner and walked into Frank's Island Café and Donut Shop. Frank came out from behind the counter, handed Jake a mug of black coffee and sat down next to him. "I know you're in the middle of Captain Manny's murder case," he began, but Jake cut him off before he could finish.

"Attempted murder case," Jake corrected and sipped the hot brew. "Manny's wife is not dead."

Frank bent over. "You mean 'not dead - *yet.*' She will be if they keep her in that motel with a view they call a hospital on the island."

"It's really not that bad. They can't move her for a few days. Afraid of more internal bleeding."

"I heard you're using Dr. Rosenbaum to get Manny off."

"Mickey Rosenbaum is seeing Manny today and the competency hearing is set for tomorrow."

"Kind of cutting it close to the bone, ain't you? And why would you be using Dr. Rosenbaum?"

"Hey, he's our local shrink. He's on-island on Thursdays and he agreed to stay another day to testify."

"You think Captain Manny was crazy when he shot his wife?"

"It's not whether he was crazy when he shot his wife. It's about his current state of mind. Whether he has sufficient mental capacity to understand the charges, make a plea and help with his defense."

Just then Jake's cell phone rang. The call was from his office. "I've got to take this, Frank. Be right back." He walked outside onto the deck while Frank sat inside at the table.

It was his paralegal, Penny Pacheco. "You're not going to like this, boss. It's a bummer for us on Alice's expert, Dr. Charles Cross."

"Do tell."

"You want the long version or the short one."

"Short will be fine."

"I learned last night the good Dr. Charles Cross is the Chairman of the Psychology Department at Yale University, on staff at Yale New Haven Hospital and wrote three books on dissociative mental disorders. He's the world's leading expert on the subject. I used our medical library account at Tufts Med School and had his books and the others you asked me to order sent over by courier. I'm going through them now and marking the pages you wanted to see. Looks like Dr. Cross is quoted everywhere in the APA Manual on dissociative mental disorders."

Jake thought out loud on the line. "Damn! Alice sandbagged us."

"Looks like."

Jake remained hopeful. "Well, all's not lost. Mickey Rosenbaum's not exactly chopped liver. He's examining Manny Campos today and will be ready for us at tomorrow's hearing."

"Hmm. That's the second problem, boss. Mickey called this morning and said he was in Miami at a medical conference and suggested you find someone else. He called from a 305 area code. That's Miami."

The news hit Jake like a bucket of ice water. "That son of a bitch promised to testify for us. And I had to pay him before he was supposed to see Manny." Then he thought a moment. "Oh, I understand it. Alice got to him. This isn't the first time she's pulled this on a defense lawyer."

"You think?"

"It's no mystery Mickey Rosenbaum told Alice we were going to rely on dissociative mental disorders. So she found the guy who wrote the book on them."

"What are you going to do?"

Jake thought a moment. "I wonder if Rosenbaum has a receptionist."

"I doubt it. I can check, but he's only here one day a week. Most of the doctors who are part-time on the island use Jimmy Dolan's answering service."

"Send the answering service a *subpoena duces tecum* for tomorrow's probable cause hearing. Summons Mickey Rosenbaum's telephone records including all written telephone messages from the last week."

"Can we subpoena them Jake? I mean, aren't they part of his patients' records and privileged communications?"

"Hey, you're beginning to sound like a lawyer. Sure, some of the calls and messages may be privileged. I'm not sure about telephone numbers and social calls. I think calls from the Alice's phone numbers and messages between Alice and Mickey are fair game. Anyways, some smartass lawyer is going to have to assert the privilege and I'm not planning on using them the way you're thinking. Alice likes to play poker. Let's see if she recognizes a bluff when she sees one."

"OK, consider it done. Until we find another psychiatrist, what about a continuance, Jake?"

"Judge McNaught is never ever going to grant us a continuance for the competency hearing. Is there another shrink on this island who can help?"

"No. Not here, maybe in Boston or on the Cape."

"Fine, I'll be in the office in ten or fifteen minutes. Compile a short list of possible psychiatrists who you think will come over to the island today or tonight to see Manny and I'll call them. In the meantime, check out Dr. Cross' text books and see if you can find anything in them we can use to impeach his testimony. But first send out the deputy sheriff to serve the summons on the answering service and then search for the shrinks."

"Jake, psychiatrists usually don't answer their phones until the end of the day. The hearing's tomorrow morning."

"Don't remind me. I'll be there in a few minutes." Jake closed the phone and looked out at the harbor for a moment. He turned back to see Frank still waiting at the table. He walked back inside. "Frank, I've got to go back to the office. It's an emergency."

Frank saw the grim look on Jake's face and tried to lighten his load. "An emergency on the Vineyard, Jake? What happened? A boat hit a lobster trap? They run out of sand on South Beach? Do you want to hear about real emergencies? I got them for you. Sit next to me for five minutes and finish your coffee. I got emergencies up the ying-yang. Employees don't show up, power failures, septic tank backups in our bathrooms. You want emergencies, I got 'em."

Jake leaned over and whispered, "Rosenbaum flew the coop."

Frank's expression changed instantly. "That's what I was trying to tell you. A while back, Rosenbaum and Alice were a number on the island."

Jake took a moment to digest the information. He thought about trying to disqualify Alice. He knew getting Alice tossed from the legal chessboard would not change the game. If she left by the back door, another prosecutor would walk in through the front door. Anyway, Jake needed to show prosecutorial misconduct.

In a deliberate tone, Jake asked, "And now what's their story?"

Frank raised his hands. "Don't know."

Jake shook his head in disbelief. "I think I do. I only wish I could prove it."

*

Jake sat nursing his second glass of scotch in the living room while Robert Paul stirred a pot of boiling linguine that sat on the stove next to a hot bowl of white clam sauce. He turned off the stovetop and deftly drained the water into the sink through a metal colander and heaped the linguine on two large plates. Then he generously parceled the clam sauce on top of the pasta.

"Come and get it, boss," he called out as he sat down and tried his masterpiece. When Jake didn't move, Robert Paul tried enticing him with a taste of guilt. "Mmm, sweet Lake Tashmoo clams," he exclaimed and dug in. "Come on Jake. I wrecked my waders this morning raking these clams at low tide."

It took all the strength he had left from the day to pull himself up from the divan. Jake wearily walked to the dinner table, putting his drink beside the plate. He sat down and just stared into space.

"Rough day, huh boss?"

Jake nodded, but said nothing to the big Wampanoag Indian.

They both sat eating in silence. After a moment, Robert Paul said, "You know the Settlement Conference is Saturday."

Jake looked puzzled. "What conference?"

"The one everyone is depending on you to win."

"When is it?"

"Saturday morning, nine o'clock. Harborside Inn, Edgartown. The Council reserved the Chilmark Room."

"Saturday morning, Harborside Inn," Jake repeated mechanically.

"Three hundred and fifty Native Americans living in Gay Head and the spirits of thousands who have gone before them and those who come hereafter are depending on you."

Jake swallowed a slug of scotch and tapped the glass. "They might do better depending on these spirits. I think I'm about washed up as an island lawyer."

"What the hell happened to you today?"

"How long we know one another, Chief?"

"Mmm. Is this going to be another one of those 'I need to get off this island' speeches of yours?"

"I need to get off this freakin' island, Chief. It's killing me."

"You cannot leave until you finish the Settlement Conference for my people. If I have to carry you inside the Harborside Inn tied to a chair, you're going to the Settlement Conference on Saturday."

"I'm not going to make it to Saturday. Saturday, hell! I am not going to get through tomorrow. This has to be my last day on the island."

"All right, tell me. What's happened?"

"I'll tell you. It's Dr. Rosenbaum. He double crossed me."

"Mmmm."

"He's in Miami Beach, doubtless waiting for Alice to come down. They're probably going to spend their nights shacked up and their days talking about dissociative mental disorders, leaving

Captain Manny and me hanging high and dry. I need to get off this island, Chief. It's killing me."

"I saw this coming. I knew it from the second you first started talking about Rosenbaum, the Harvard shrink. What are you planning to do?"

"What am I going to do? First, I know I'm not driving over to that poker game tonight. I might just strangle Alice Wishansky. No, strangling's too good for her. I'm going to take the power boat over to Shark Bay, put her feet in the water for bait and let the sharks work on her."

"The power boat's in the shed, Jake."

"All right, forget Alice, I'm getting off this island tonight. If I'm not in court in the morning, they'll have to continue the case and Manny's sure to get another lawyer. He can look for a psychiatrist, 'cause I failed miserably today."

Jake's house phone rang and Robert Paul rose from the table and picked up the phone in the kitchen. "Mr. Dellahunt's residence, Robert Paul speaking. Yes, mmm, uh-huh, OK, uh-huh, OK, sure, yes. Got it. Thank you for calling. I'll tell him."

He hung up the phone and returned to the table. He smiled at Jake without a word, sat down and began slurping up pasta.

"Are you going to stuff your face or tell me what that was all about?"

"Jake Dellahunt, do you know what I love the most about you?"

"Let me guess. My incredible good looks?"

"You are the luckiest son of bitch on this island. Always have been and always will be. And Lady Luck is smiling on you tonight."

Jake sat up straight. "Is the Chief of Psychiatry at Harvard Med School coming to testify for us?"

"Better."

"Mmm, A shark actually swallowed Alice Wishansky?"

"You are getting warmer."

"OK, I give up."

"That was Mr. Sullivan, the clerk of the District Court in Edgartown. Seems like tonight's poker game was cancelled."

"Is that all? Hell, I wasn't planning to go to the poker game. Would have probably killed Alice. I'm packing a bag and leaving this God-forsaken island."

"Don't you want to know why your card game was cancelled?"

"I'll bite. Sure, why?"

"Judge McNaught and his wife were driving back from an early dinner at the Homeport Restaurant in Menemsha, when they had an auto accident."

"How are they?"

"Mr. Sullivan says he's got a few cuts and scrapes, but his wife's been injured bad. Judge is staying with her at the Vineyard Hospital."

"Thanks to Cheezus!"

"Mr. Sullivan says you and Alice both are to come to court tomorrow morning with your expert doctor witnesses just in case, but he is pretty sure Captain Manny's case will be continued for a couple of weeks."

*

The next morning, Robert Paul waited in the cottage driveway. His black hair was combed and braided neatly and he was dressed in a clean pair of blue jeans and a brown suit jacket with sleeves so short his arms stuck out of them. He wore his best Western dress shirt and a bolo string tie with an oval, green sea-coral tie clip.

Jake came running out of the house and hollered, "Have you seen the keys to the truck anywhere?"

The big Indian did not reply. Instead, he waited until Jake reached him and then opened the passenger's door to Jake's Ford 150 pickup truck. He waived the keys to the truck in his gigantic hand and said, "Get in."

Jake shook his head. "I may have a bit of a hangover this morning, but I'm perfectly capable of driving myself over to the Edgartown Courthouse, Chief."

"Orders are not to let you out of my sight until I deliver you to the Harborside Inn Settlement Conference tomorrow."

"You got orders? Aren't you supposed to be working for me?"

"Sure boss. Sure. But sometimes the Tribal Council takes orders from the Great Spirit and then they send me along to enforce 'em. Now to please get inside and I will drive you to the office to get your lawyer bag."

"You know kidnapping an officer of the court is a crime, don't you?"

"No, I am just helping you. You are really beloved by our people, Jake. The Tribal Council appreciates your help so much, they asked me to make one stop up-island. They have a fine gift for you. So, please get in."

"A gift for me? Maybe they should wait until *after* the Settlement Conference. They may not be so generous."

"Inside," Robert Paul ordered, pointing his burly index finger in the direction of the passenger seat.

Jake figured the Indian to be about six-five and three hundred pounds. He got into the truck without another word.

Fifteen minutes later they reached Lighthouse Road in Gay Head and pulled over to the side of the road. A small Wampanoag Indian, neatly dressed in a tie, shirt and a newly pressed blue suit climbed into the truck bed behind the cab.

"Isn't that Little Franny Meezum?"

"Mmmm," Robert Paul nodded.

"What's he doing on the back of my truck?"

"He's the gift. Just in case you need an expert to testify today."

"Great."

"You're welcome."

*

Jake thought it peculiar the small courtroom in Edgartown was filled with spectators. He wondered if they had not heard about Judge McNaught's accident and made the trip to the courthouse for nothing. Jake sat at the defense table between Manny Campos and his paralegal and across from Alice and her expert. Penny had stacked a pile of medical books on the defense table including the three books the prosecutor's expert had written. He glanced at Alice, but she looked straight ahead, refusing to acknowledge he was in the courtroom. One way or another, she would be going to the woodshed.

Jake sized up Alice Wishansky's expert, Dr. Charles Cross. He seemed emaciated to Jake. Dressed in an old, dark woolen three piece suit, he reminded Jake of pictures of Sigmund Freud he had seen in textbooks. He was a small, painfully lean man, thin faced, with a pair of thick, silver, metal-rimmed glasses, a trimmed gray beard and mustache and thinning gray hair. Jake glanced behind the rail. Robert Paul sat next to a number of members of the Tribal Council including the passenger they brought to the hearing, Little Franny Meezum. When they saw Jake looking at them, they all waved and nodded as if they were at a picnic and he was bringing them dessert.

Jake studied the score of somber judges' black and white wooden-framed photos that looked down unhappily from the drab walls. It was fifteen minutes past the normal session hour of ten o'clock when the Clerk of the District Court, Mr. Sullivan, walked in and stood behind the clerk's bench. Jake sat up straight and waited for him to set the new date for the continuance. The spectators grew quiet. Just at the very moment he expected the announcement, out of the corner of his eye, Jake saw Judge McNaught sauntering into the courtroom. In an instant, the Judge stood in front of the bench bigger than life. Jake felt his heart rate double. While everyone else stood up and the clerk spieled out his hear ye's, Jake remained seated and could be heard saying, "Oh shit. I'm dead."

After everyone sat down, the Judge turned to Jake and said, "Is there reason you did not rise to your feet in respect for this court, Mr. Dellahunt?"

Jake jumped to his feet. "I had heard you were in an accident Your Honor and would not be in court this morning. I was so surprised to see you I was in shock. That's all."

"I wouldn't be here this morning if not for some good Samaritans who stopped to give us first aid. And tell, me Mr. Dellahunt, when I came into the courtroom what did you shout out?"

"I was so pleased to see you, I said, 'oh sure glad you're not dead.'"

"Well, so am I," the Judge replied and the gallery laughed. "Alright then, I believe you called for this competency hearing so I will hear from your expert first, Dr. Rosenbaum."

"He's not here."

"Where is he?"

"He's been delayed."

"Do you want to put on another expert?"

"If the court will take Dr. Cross, the Commonwealth's expert witness out of order, we might save some time."

"In that case, since Dr. Cross is present and ready, I will hear from Ms. Wishansky's expert first."

Jake sat down and breathed a momentary sigh of relief.

After Dr. Cross was sworn, Alice began to establish Dr. Cross' qualifications as an expert in the field of psychology. "Please tell the court where you went to school, the dates you graduated and your degrees and honors?"

"Princeton University, BS Degree, 1975, Phi Beta Kappa, Summa cum Laude and Yale University, PhD Degree in Psychology in 1980."

"Where are you currently employed?"

"I hold the Alden C. Chapman Chair of Clinical Psychology at Yale University New Haven Medical School and serve as Chairman of the Department of Psychology at Yale University."

"Publications in the field?"

"I have written over three hundred papers that have been published in various medical journals and have written three books on dissociative mental disorders."

"Have you examined Mr. Campos?"

"Yes, I spent an hour with him yesterday."

"Did you form an opinion as to whether Mr. Campos is sufficiently competent to stand trial, he understands the nature and consequences of these proceedings, and he understands these proceedings well enough to answer the charges against him and assist his counsel in preparing a defense?"

"I do have an opinion."

"And what is your opinion, Dr. Cross?"

"He is competent to stand trial."

"And what do you base your opinion upon?"

"I base my opinion on my psychological examination of the defendant, his medical history, the hundreds of books and thousands of case histories I have read and conducted, my thirty years of clinical experience and my knowledge in the field of psychology. I found Mr. Campos was able to answer questions coherently and responsively. On the whole, I found him to be mentally aware of his surroundings and his situation. I believe he understands the charges, these proceedings, and is sufficiently mentally aware to assist in preparing his defense. I am of the opinion he is competent to stand trial."

Alice looked over to Jake. "You may inquire."

Jake stood up holding a book in his hand. "Dr. Cross, are you a licensed psychologist in Massachusetts?"

"No, but I am licensed in 29 other states."

"But not in the Commonwealth."

"No, not here."

"And you are not a physician with any medical degree?"

"No, I have a PhD degree in psychology."

"When you were qualified as an expert, you stated you wrote three books on dissociative mental disorders. Do you recognize the book I am holding?"

"Yes, it's *Signs and Symptoms of Dissociative Disorders*, the leading textbook on diagnosing and treating the illness. I wrote the book."

"Could you define the term, dissociative disorders?"

"Objection."

Judge McNaught said, "You know the rule, Mr. Dellahunt. You may not use the Commonwealth's expert to put in an opinion. You must use your own expert to give opinion evidence."

"This is not opinion evidence. It's limited to a definition only."

"I'll give you some latitude, but do not abuse the rule. Objection overruled. You may answer the question if you can, Doctor."

"Yes, dissociative disorders are marked by a dissociation from or interruption of a person's fundamental aspects of the waking consciousness."

"In plain English, Doctor."

"Dissociative disorders generally change one's perception of reality, identity, memory and personal history."

"What causes the dissociative disorders?"

Alice was on her feet once again. "Same Objection, Your Honor. The rule is clear the defense cannot offer expert opinion from our expert."

The judge seemed vexed. "Objection sustained. I am warning you, Mr. Dellahunt. You may not ask this expert for opinions. You can only elicit expert opinions from your own expert when you put your own expert on the witness stand. You know the rule."

Jake knew the rule only too well. He moved toward the witness stand and placed the doctor's book on the stand. "I'll rephrase my question. In your textbook, 'Signs and Symptoms of Dissociative

Disorders,' please turn to page 44 which I have marked and please read the highlighted version to the court."

"Objection."

The judge turned to Alice and said, "Overruled. Anything in the book is valid cross-examination since your expert testified he wrote the book. The contents are fair game. You may proceed, Mr. Dellahunt."

Dr. Cross began reading out loud from the book. "All dissociative disorders are thought to stem from trauma experienced by an individual with this disorder. The dissociative aspect is thought to be a coping mechanism. The person literally dissociates himself from a situation or experience too traumatic to integrate with his conscious self."

"When you examined Mr. Campos, did he tell you about his ordeal battling gales on his fishing boat for four days and three nights, eventually losing his boat, most of his crew drowning, being thrown into the frigid sea for hours and nearly drowning himself?"

"Yes, he did relate that to me."

"Did you consider that experience could be 'too traumatic to integrate with his conscious self?'"

"Anything could be, but I did not believe that to be true."

"Do you believe he suffers or suffered from a dissociative disorder as a result of those traumatic events?"

"No, I don't."

"Despite the trauma he suffered?"

"Not every traumatic event triggers a dissociative disorder, Mr. Dellahunt."

"And Dr. Cross, again, did you consider the situation of being immersed in frigid sea water for hours, hundreds of miles from land, to be an experience or a situation too traumatic to integrate with his conscious self?"

"No, I did not believe that to be true either."

"And did you take into account the shooting occurred the very night, within minutes of the time Mr. Campos returned home from sea?"

"I did."

"Do you agree he suffered a serious trauma at sea just before he came home?"

"Yes."

"But you do not believe it created a dissociative disorder?"

"I can only say I believe he does not presently suffer from any dissociative disorder."

"So he may have suffered dissociation at the time of the shooting."

"Quite possibly. I don't know. I was asked to examine his current state of mind."

Jake could see cracks beginning to appear in Cross' testimony. "So you're saying he could have been suffering a mental disease at the time of the shooting, but he's as healthy as a horse now."

The spectators began to laugh and the judge banged down his gavel and warned them he would clear the courtroom should there be another outburst.

Jake continued to hammer away. "Please turn to page 87 of your book which I have marked and please read the highlighted version to the court."

Doctor Cross cleared his throat and began slowly. "Dissociative Amnesia Disorder is characterized by a blocking out of critical personal information, usually of a traumatic or stressful nature. Dissociative Amnesia, unlike other types of amnesia, does not result from other medical trauma, such as a blow to the head. It is characterized by memory loss of specific events that took place, usually traumatic."

"Thank you Doctor. You may put the book down. When you examined Mr. Campos, did he describe the shooting to you?"

"I never asked him about what happened in the house."

"So you cannot state whether Mr. Campos suffers from a present memory loss of the events that occurred in the house?"

"Objection," Alice growled.

The judge fired back, "Overruled. It's a factual question. You may answer."

"I cannot answer that question because I don't know. I can only say such amnesia is rarely permanent and is a transient disorder."

"Dr. Cross, did you consider a depersonalization disorder in forming your opinion?"

"Yes. It is not a case of depersonalization."

Jake thought Dr. Cross answered the question too quickly, a sure sign he did not want to get into it. "Would you define it?"

Alice was on her feet again. "Objection."

Judge McNaught was clearly becoming chafed with Jake. "The objection is sustained. I warned you, Mr. Dellahunt. The next time you ask a question that calls for an opinion based on the expert's knowledge, I am going to hold you in contempt."

"I apologize, Your Honor," Jake said.

Jake returned to the defense table and picked up a large text book. "Are you acquainted with the American Psychology Association's *Diagnostic and Statistical Manual of Mental Disorders*?"

"Of course."

"Would you consider it a learned treatise on psychology?"

"I suppose so, yes."

"I move this text be admitted into evidence as a learned treatise."

"Any objection, Ms. Wishansky?" asked Judge McNaught.

Alice responded, "None, Your Honor."

Jake moved toward the witness. "Please read the highlighted area on page 474 of the manual."

Dr. Cross read aloud. "A depersonalization disorder is marked by feeling out of control of one's actions and movements and is something people describe when intoxicated. An individual with depersonalization disorder has this experience so severely it interrupts his or her functioning and experience."

Jake put the pedal to the metal and repeated the last phrase Cross had read to be sure the judge heard it. "'Interrupts his or her functioning and experience.' Again I ask you, in forming your opinion, did you ever consider whether Mr. Campos suffered or currently suffers from a depersonalization disorder?"

"I did and he does not suffer from a depersonalization deficit."

"One last question, you're an expert on dissociative disorders, right?"

"Yes."

"Do you know why an expert on dissociative disorders was chosen to testify at this hearing, if in fact Mr. Campos is not suffering from a dissociative disorder?"

"Objection."

"Withdrawn."

Jake had run out of questions. "That's all I have for cross-examination, Your Honor."

"Do you have anything on re-cross, Ms. Wishansky?"

"No, Your Honor."

The judge rose. "Then we stand adjourned for thirty minutes for morning recess and when we return, we will take Mr. Dellahunt's expert."

Jake sat down and waited for the courtroom to clear. Manny was taken from the courtroom and after a while, Penny and Jake sat alone in the courtroom. "You certainly gave the judge something to think about, boss. I mean he's got to be thinking about mental disease now."

"We barely dented a fender. We need an expert to wreck the rest of the body of the Dr. Cross' testimony. Judge McNaught might be thinking Manny could be incompetent, but if we can't offer some solid testimony he is incompetent, we'll lose and Manny will be going to trial."

"What about calling his daughter? She saw him that night."

Jake shook his head. "Did anyone show up from the answering service?"

"Yes, the owner. Mr. James Dolan himself and he has the records."

"Did you see them?"

Although they were alone in the courtroom, Penny leaned over and whispered in Jake's ear, "I shouldn't be telling you this, but James Dolan is my godfather. He swore me to secrecy. He said there wasn't anything that could help us in the phone records and Alice has been asking him about them. He told her he's holding onto them until the court decides if they're to be admitted. "

"Ah, Alice is going to object. Good."

"That's good?"

"Yeah, it will be perfect."

"What's perfect if there's nothing in them?"

"She doesn't know that. We do. It's a poker game, isn't it?"

Jake put his arms on the table, closed his eyes and rested his head on them. He heard the words come out of his mouth, but could hardly believe he uttered them. "What do you think about calling Little Franny Meezum as our expert?"

"You crazy? He's the Wampanoag Tribal Shaman."

"I'm not crazy, just desperate."

*

The courtroom fell silent when Jake stood up and declared, "Call Dr. Francis Meezum to the stand."

Little Franny moved from his seat in the back of the courtroom, was sworn in and sat in the witness box. The courtroom became so quiet Jake could hear his heart beating.

"What is your full name?"

"Francis Xavier Red-Dog Meezum."

"Are you employed?"

"Yes, I am the Wampanoag Tribal Shaman."

"What does that mean?"

"I am a holistic healer and doctor to 350 Wampanoag and many more White People who come to me to be healed."

"Did you go to school to become a Shaman?"

"I did not start out to become a Native American Shaman. I was chosen by the Tribal Council to apply for a scholarship to Phillips Exeter Academy in New Hampshire. They accepted me and after graduating from Exeter, I was invited to attend Dartmouth College to fill their land grant quota for Native Americans. It was a free education. I received a BS Degree from Dartmouth in psychology in 1995."

Jake could not believe his ears. Little Franny was either a genius or the best damned liar in the tribe. Either way, everyone in the courtroom, including the Judge, was glued to his every word.

"You went to Dartmouth?"

"Yup, and I graduated first in my class."

"And after graduating from College, where did you go?"

"Two years at Mary Hitchcock Medical School at Dartmouth and then five years studying holistic medicine in various places around the world."

"Can you name a few?"

"In the Andes in Peru with Shaman Quechua, Grupo Osanimi with rainforest people in Ecuador, Foundation for Shaman Study in Oregon, Red Cloud's Holistic Medical Research Foundation in the Southwest, and three years in Tibet studying with Holy Lama and Medical Doctor Tenzhang Yeshe."

"Did you receive any degree?"

"No degree is yet offered or recognized in the United States, but I am a certified Native American Doctor of Holistic Medicine."

"Do you know and have you visited with the defendant?"

"I have known Manny Campos for many years. I spent the past few days talking with him and trying to heal him."

Jake turned to the Judge. "I offer Dr. Meezum be accepted as an expert in mental health."

The Judge looked at Alice. "What say you, Ms. Wishansky?"

"I object to his qualifications. He's not qualified to render any expert opinion about the defendant's mental health. He hasn't the education or training to be considered an expert in psychology or psychiatry. He isn't even a doctor. For God's sake, he's an Indian medicine man. Please do not allow this man to palm himself off as some kind of doctor. He lives in a teepee with a bunch of howling dogs."

Jake looked at the Judge without a saying a word.

Judge McNaught thoughtfully responded. "Ms. Wishansky, it doesn't matter where or how a man chooses to live. I would point out your expert was not a medical doctor either. His copy-cat Freudian dress and look this morning did not go unnoticed. Maybe he thinks looking and dressing like Freud will increase his persuasiveness with this court."

"Maybe so, but at least Dr. Cross has a legitimate doctorate degree in psychology."

"Both experts have degrees in psychology and Dr. Meezum not only went to medical school for two years, but also spent five years studying to become a Shaman. I think we can call him an expert."

"At what? The spirit world?"

Judge McNaught banged his gavel. "Sit down Ms. Wishansky. I know about this man's healing power first hand. He was the good Samaritan who helped me and saved my wife from bleeding to death last night. So, let's move on. I find Dr. Meezum eminently qualified to render expert opinion in this case."

*

It took little more than fifteen minutes for Jake and Little Franny Meezum to convince Judge McNaught that Captain Manny Campos was suffering from a depersonalization disorder and was incompetent to stand trial. The Judge made his ruling from the bench and sent Manny to Bridgewater State Hospital for treatment until such time as he was well enough to stand trial.

Before the Judge closed the proceedings, Jake stood up and addressed the court. "I have one more matter before the court. It's a matter of possible prosecutorial misconduct."

"Maybe we had better hear that in chambers," Judge McNaught suggested.

"I have summonsed Dr. Rosenbaum's telephone records for you to examine."

Alice rose to her feet. "I object to opening the records. They are part of patients' medical records and are privileged materials."

Jake looked at her. Her Cheshire cat grin had disappeared and she was beginning to sweat. Jake then said, "I suggest Your Honor examine the records 'in camera,' while we're at lunch." It was an old trick to get the court to see the records first to determine if they were indeed privileged. Of course, Jake knew the judge would find nothing in the records, but Alice didn't.

"We'll take the matter up after lunch. Court orders subpoenaed records held for two o'clock argument." The Judge banged his gavel and closed the Probable Cause Hearing.

After Jake thanked Little Franny, he asked, "Do you think Captain Manny will recover quickly?"

"You asking for my professional opinion?"

"Sure."

"As I told the Judge, Manny is suffering from a depersonalization deficit. The sea took his boat and killed most of his crew. He personified the sea as the woman he loved. In traumatic shock, his mind displaced his wife with the sea and he struck back. When he recognizes the displacement occurred and the reality of the events, he will recover. That may take months or years. If that is all Mr. Dellahunt, I have patients to see today."

*

Penny packed up a load of books and file cases on a two-wheeler and left. After a while, the spectators trickled out of the courtroom leaving only Jake and Alice seated at their tables. Neither spoke a word for a long time.

Alice began. "What do you want Jake?"

"When Manny is well, I want your assurance he won't be tried for murder if she dies or attempted murder if she doesn't."

"What else?"

"The state is supposed to pay defense attorney's fees and expenses for indigent defendants in murder cases. I just found out the defense fund is as broke as Manny. I want the DA's office to pay me five grand for law services and two grand more for Dr. Meezum's expert testimony."

"Seven thousand? For what? The answering service telephone records are privileged and can't be used against me."

"You want to bet your ticket to practice law on it? I'll be happy to accommodate you."

"You have no idea what's in those records."

"Maybe so, but if you called Dr. Rosenbaum in the last two or three days, I have a pretty good idea the call records will reflect your telephone numbers, call frequency and the length of time of your conversations."

"You'll never get those records opened."

Jake walked up to Alice. He put on his best poker face as he spit out the words. "Let's cut the crap, Alice. You hired a dissociative disease expert before I ever set up a dissociative disorder defense. Rosenbaum opened our defense to you. You agreed to the three days because you sent Rosenberg to Miami, knowing I would never have enough time to find a replacement. You should have told the court about your relationship with Mickey. He'll eventually crack and you are going so far down, hell will only be the first stop. So I'm walking out of here in ten seconds unless you agree to set this straight."

Alice thought about it for all of two seconds and folded. "Alright. But the seven thousand will have to come out of the DA's discretionary fund."

Jake thought about the two IRS collection agents running around the island. "No checks, Alice. I want cash. And tell Mickey

Rosenbaum, I want him to return the two grand I gave him last week to testify. Otherwise, he's going down with you."

"You know Jake, you're working for the wrong side as a criminal defense lawyer."

"I don't think so. When can I have the nine grand?"

"I'll have the cash over to your office this afternoon with a letter of understanding about Manny Campos. Is that soon enough?"

After lunch, Jake handed Judge McNaught a handwritten agreement to dismiss the claim of prosecutorial misconduct. The judge turned to Alice. "I know exactly what went down Alice. If you ever send any more defense witnesses on vacations to Miami, I am going to file a complaint against you with the Board of Bar Overseers. We all live and work on an island together. Let's not act like the lawyers on the mainland. That's America. This is paradise. Now I want both of you to shake hands and promise only to be adversarial at Thursday night's weekly poker game."

*

It was just 6:00 AM on Saturday morning when Jake's cell phone rang. Jake fumbled for the phone on his bedside table, opened it and mumbled a hello.

"I didn't have any chance to thank you yesterday, Mr. Dellahunt."

Jake rubbed his eyes. "What the hell time is it?"

"It's time to wake up, Mr. Dellahunt. Did you know they have telephones at Bridgewater State for patients to call anywhere they like? Even their lawyers on Martha's Vineyard?"

"Who is this?"

"This is your Portuguese fisherman client sending you a wake-up call."

Jake recognized the voice. "Manny, Manny Campos. What in God's name are you talking about? What wake-up call?"

"Did you know my wife was banging someone while I was away? I was out at sea, risking my life every day and she was screwing some guy. My kid called me on the boat's radio phone. I'm sure you saw the guy driving up and down Cottage Road every night."

"What the hell are you talking about?"

"You can't ever repeat this conversation to anyone because you're my lawyer. Right?"

Jake sat up. "No, I can't tell anyone. It's a privileged lawyer-client communication. Wait a minute. Are you saying you knew what you were doing when you shot your wife?"

"And you lapped up all that stuff about 'the sea she be a beautiful woman.'"

"You shot her because she was unfaithful? You've been faking your condition all along?"

Manny's voice sounded momentarily deranged. "'Do you really think you're just buying fish, Mr. Dellahunt? You're not just paying for a piece of fish. You're buying pieces of men's lives.' Pretty good stuff, huh?"

"You lying son of a bitch."

"I seemed to have recovered, Mr. Dellahunt. Don't be too hard on me. You did such a great job, I want to hire you to get me out of Bridgewater. Now that I have come back to my senses, I want to go back and finish the job."

Jake closed the phone without another word. From the very beginning of his days in courtrooms, Jake knew everybody lied. Defendants, witnesses, prosecutors, and lawyers - they all lied. But this was too much. He thought about being used by Manny Campos. He didn't like it and this wasn't going to be the end of it.

*

Robert Paul drove Jake to Frank's Island Café and Donut Shop and waited for him to pick up two cups of coffee before leaving for Settlement Conference. "You did a great job for Manny," Frank said as he poured the coffee into the two large cups and threw three dozen assorted donuts in a large plastic bag.

Jake didn't respond to the compliment. He was in a grumpy mood. "I didn't ask for all these donuts this morning."

"On the house, counselor."

Jake left the shop carrying two coffee cups and the bag of donuts. He handed the big Wampanoag a coffee and the bag of donuts as he got into the truck.

The Chief opened the bag and peeked inside. "Hey, who's all these donuts for?"

"We're going to bribe the federal mediators with donuts."

Jake and Robert Paul drove onto Main Street and parked in front of the Grapes of Wrath bookstore. They stepped out of the truck and climbed the stairs to Jake's law offices to gather the few notes and other materials Jake had quickly put together for the Settlement Conference.

Penny was waiting inside and handed Jake an envelope. "Alice dropped this off late yesterday afternoon."

Jake sipped his coffee and opened it. It contained two copies of an "Agreement to Forbear from Prosecution of Manuel J. Campos" and nine thousand dollars in cash. Alice had signed the agreement.

He handed the money to the Chief. "Count this out and make sure there's nine thousand in the stash. Put two thousand in an envelope and give it to Little Franny for his testimony."

Jake turned around to Penny. "Put back the two thousand we gave Rosenbaum in the safe. I want you to give the rest, our five grand in fees, to Maria Medeiros at the Stone Bank. Have her put it in a mutual fund for Manny's daughter's education."

Penny eyed the overdue office bills sitting on the windowsill behind Jake's desk. "We could use some of that money to pay bills."

"I know, but so could Manny's daughter. Look, we have a big fee coming in next week from the Wampanoag Tribe for settling their land case. Right Chief?"

"I never asked how much you are going to charge."

"Have I ever asked the Tribe for money? My fee will be a trifling percentage of the gross taken in by the Wampanoag Indian Casino."

"We do not have a casino, boss."

"Not now, but you will after the Settlement Conference."

Penny and the Robert Paul just smiled and shook their heads. They both knew Jake was a dreamer. That's why so many people on the island loved him and that number included the two people in the room with Jake. Penny started to unlock the office safe. "Did you hear Manny's wife is out of Intensive Care? They think she will make a full recovery. Turns out Manny was a lousy shot. Only one bullet hit her."

Robert Paul put Franny's envelope in his pocket and gave the rest of the money and the agreements not to prosecute to Penny to lock up in the office safe. "The count is right and I'm holding Little Franny Meezum's fee."

Jake took the agreements from Penny. "I've changed my mind on DA's Agreements Not to Prosecute. Call Alice first thing Monday morning, tell her I have withdrawn my representation effective last night. She can do whatever she wants when Manny's released from Bridgewater. I'm not signing the agreement."

Penny looked shocked. "You serious, boss?

Jake pushed the agreements into the shredder and turned it on. "Is this serious enough for you?" He watched the papers disappear into the machine and waited a few moments before turning toward the two of them.

Penny shook her head and solemnly asked, "I don't understand. Why?"

"Let's just say, justice has been done."

He felt good about the morning's events. He smiled and said, "OK, let's go people. The United States is waiting for us. It would be unpatriotic to make them wait a minute more for us to take their money."

Chapter Two

The Case of the Dead Dog

It was a sky blue island morning with the promise of a spring thaw in the air that persuaded Jake to go into the office earlier than usual. It wasn't because he was particularly busy. He wasn't. Most of Jake's law business left on the ferry after Labor Day weekend and wasn't coming back until Memorial Day.

The winter months had whittled Jake's caseload inventory down to a case of trespass on private property, a theft of twelve lobster traps, a case of shoplifting Black Dog T-shirts from the Island Dry Goods and Sundries Shop, one peeping Tom case, three cases of assaulting naked girls on Lucy Vincent Beach in Chilmark, a taxi license application, a driving under the influence charge, one housebreak, three speeding tickets, one dog bite case and a pair of pending personal injury claims as a result of a moped collision in front of Hall's Up-Island Market in West Tisbury. Real estate was the most lucrative law work on the island but the part-time Dukes County Island Prosecutor and Assistant District Attorney, Skeeter McLain held the monopoly on all the real estate law business on the island.

The cottage on Lake Tashmoo Jake inherited from Judge Sam Mathews was only a ten minute walk to his office above Grapes of Wrath bookstore. On the way to work that morning, he stopped at the Tisbury Post Office and picked up the mail. He sat down in his office and dismissively looked at the two envelopes he received in the mail from the IRS marked, "Urgent Request Requires Immediate Response." Without opening them, he stuffed the envelopes in the bottom drawer of his desk with all of the other urgent requests. Then he turned in his chair and tossed the other bills on top of a growing stack on the windowsill directly behind him. Jake never worried much about bills until they were piled so high he couldn't see out the window anymore.

Just as he finished "sorting" the mail, the phone rang.

"Dellahunt office," he answered pretending to be the Penny Pacheco, his paralegal-receptionist-secretary, who only worked three days a week.

"Is lawyah Dellahunt there?" the voice asked in a distinct down-east inflection.

"Who's calling?" Jake asked in a secretarial tone.

"I've called a couple of other lawyahs in the phone book and they suggested I speak to him."

"About what?"

"I'd rathah not say."

"I've got to tell Mr. Dellahunt why you're calling."

"Ask him if he reads the Vineyard Gazette. Tell him I'm the chicken farmah. He'll know what it's about."

Jake's voice dropped two octaves. "Cheezus, are you John Anderson, the guy with all those chicken coops? You're plastered all over the island newspapers. You've even made it into the Cape Cod Times. You're the one who . . ."

"You Mistah Dellahunt?"

"Yes and are you the one they've got splashed all over the Vineyard Gazette?"

"That's what I want to talk about."

50

"Can you come to the office, Mr. Anderson? I don't want to talk about this on the phone."

"The staties pinched me and I'm in the county lock-up. I need a lawyah to bail me out. You know, someone to talk to the district attorney."

"You mean Skeeter McLain. What did he charge you with?"

"Animal cruelty, aggravated criminal assault, attempted murder and criminal trespass."

"What did ya tell the police?"

"Just that I wanted to speak to a lawyah."

"Good, don't say anything to the cops. I'll be over to arrange bail after I speak to Skeeter."

"Thank Jesus."

"Don't be thankin' Jesus, Mr. Anderson. If I take your case and that's a big 'if,' I'll need a twenty five thousand dollar retainer against fees of $300 an hour plus all expenses," Jake said while eyeballing his bills on the windowsill. "And Mr. Anderson, that retainer is due as soon as you walk out of jail."

The chicken farmer replied angrily "Seems like an awful lot of money for just killin' some neighborhood dog."

"You're right, it is a lot of money," Jake shot back. "But then someone cut off the dog's head and shoved it inside its owner's mailbox. That makes it a twenty five thousand dollar case. You know Mr. Anderson, it's a lot easier to get away with killing a human being on this island than killing a dog and then stuffing its head into a mailbox." Jake paused, but Anderson said nothing. "That's the fee," Jake added. "Take it or leave it." Then Jake hung up.

Jake kicked up his feet on the desk and waited. No more than a minute later, the phone rang again. It was Anderson. "I'll take it. Just get me out of this mess."

*

Jake Dellahunt waited on the deck of the Frank's Island Café and Donut Shop, working on his third cup of coffee and tasting the first hint of spring. He leaned against the weathered wooden railing, watching the mid-morning ferry arrive at the Vineyard Haven ferry station. The ferry slipped alongside the pilings and settled against the dock, its two steel doors groaning open like the mouth of a giant beached whale, but instead of spewing up its contents from the depths of the sea, it heaved up a line of trucks and cars from the mainland. A few moments later, a string of day trippers scampered off a portside companionway, down a broad steel ramp and headed toward the tourist traps on Main Street. Jake heard footsteps behind him and turned from watching the ferry to see Francis Falcone walking toward him.

"Sorry to interrupt your coffee break, counselor," said the owner of Frank's café. He was a heavy set, dark skinned, forty year-old native New Yorker with jet black hair and the beefy facial features of Luca Brasi, a character right out of a Mario Puzzo novel. Frank had owned the Vineyard Haven Café and Donut Shop for two and half years and when he bought it, he hired Jake to negotiate the deal and draft the agreements.

Jake drained the last of the coffee from the mug and then leaned his back and elbows on the deck railing. "Aren't you supposed to be in the kitchen making the donuts, Frank?"

"Made them fresh this morning. Aren't you supposed to be working in your office?"

"But I am working. You hear most of the scuttlebutt on the island. What do you know about John Anderson, the up-island chicken farmer?"

"The one in the newspapers?"

Jake nodded.

"I know two things. He inherited a 500-acre farm sitting on one prime piece of real estate overlooking the ocean in Chilmark. He's been offered thirty million for the property, but won't sell. I also know they're going to lock him up for mutilating some kid's dog and when they do, they're going to throw away the key." Frank looked at the expression on Jake's face. "Oh no, don't tell me!"

Jake nodded once again.

"You didn't take on that crazy chicken farmer for a client?"

"Thinkin' about it."

"My advice is to run in the opposite direction. He's got the whole island wanting to tow him ten miles past the Nantucket Light Ship and leave him tied to a cross, Wampanoag Indian style. Is that why you're here? To talk to me about John Anderson?"

"No, I'm actually here to have coffee and then make a short trip over to the jail in Edgartown to speak to Anderson. Then I plan to dash back here to talk to Mr. Greenpants."

"Skeeter McLain?"

"He's the island prosecutor in the case and he's nuts about wearing green pants. You didn't happen to bring me a donut, did you?"

"No, Jake. You're on the sugar wagon, remember your diet?"

"Juries love lawyers with a bit of meat on their bones. Makes them look more substantial and credible, if that's possible. Remember Clarence Darrow and our own Flea Bailey? They weren't bags of bones. Bet both ate a couple of donuts a day."

"I'll bring you a donut if that's what you want, but first I've a quick question for you, counselor."

Jake thought Frank was going to take another run at him for a case Frank had sent him. He anticipated Frank's question and headed it off. "I told you a half dozen times Frank, I can't give you anything on the accident case you sent me last year, if that's what you're looking for. Go to law school and when you're a member of the bar, I'll be glad pay you for cases you send over and work on with me."

"How about a favor then?"

"Depends. Favors I've got aplenty."

"Not much of a favor. Just make a quick call to the Massachusetts Department of Public Utilities in Boston."

"Lawyers bill time for their calls and they don't make quick ones. What's the state DPU want with you?"

"Nothing, Jake. Really nothing," Frank replied.

Jake knew better. Frank was always asking to get him out of a jam. "Come on, what does the DPU want with you, Frank?" Jake asked suspiciously.

Frank bent over close to Jake. "They say I put a couple of magnets on the electric meters in the donut shop. Why would I do that?" Frank asked in his best choirboy voice.

"To slow the kilowatt hours and save a few bucks?"

Frank thought a moment. "So, say I did stick a couple of small magnets on the meters. Not that I did anything like that. But if I did, what then?"

"It's a felony, a larceny punishable by nickel up to a dime in the can along with a heavy fine. Did they send a demand letter?"

Without answering, Frank fished a letter out of his pocket and handed it to Jake. Jake read the letter and then focused on the three main items the DPU wanted: "First, full restitution for the last two and half years of stolen electric power in the amount $11,500 plus interest, second, payment to be made promptly within 30 days, and lastly a plea of guilty to a charge of larceny." The Mass DPU was throwing the book at the native New Yorker.

"Is there anything to this DPU business you haven't told me?"

"No, nothing. I swear I didn't touch the meters."

"Maybe you didn't, but I think you forgot to tell me something."

"Yeah, what's that, Jake?"

Jake looked Frank in the eyes and chose his words carefully. "Francis, you wouldn't know an electric meter from a lawn mower. You're from the Big Apple, remember? You grew up and lived in mid-town Manhattan, a place where they don't have meters in apartments or lawns to mow. And all you know about magnets is sticking them on your refrigerator door. So tell me, who really attached the magnets to your meter and how much did you pay him? If you want me to call the Department of Public Utilities, then I want his name."

*

After Jake had agreed to speak to the Department of Public Utilities, he sat down on the deck watching the parade of islanders and day trippers continue to pass by his perch on the deck of the Frank's shop. One passenger in particular caught his attention. She was a stunning woman in high heels, wearing movie-star sunglasses and an expensive, full-length fur coat. Lots of celebs and movie stars on the island, he thought. She moved effortlessly through the crowd toward him, stopping directly on the sidewalk alongside the café deck and looked up at him. She peeled off her sun glasses as if to bring Jake closer and carefully measured him.

He looked down at her from the deck. Nobody but Maggie Dellahunt, Jake's ex-wife would wear a fur coat and heels on the Vineyard. She stayed frozen in place and expressionless, never giving away any hint of genuine feelings. Whatever she saw in his face remained an enigma to him. Maggie was older, but still as extravagantly dazzling as the first day he had met her. They looked at one another for a long moment, sizing each other up like two fighters in their opening round. Love sometimes comes and goes, but feelings never leave and Jake felt the heat rising in his body. He was surprised by the feelings. He still wanted her.

*

The Dukes County House of Correction is a large, white colonial house indistinguishable from dozens of other large, white colonial clapboard houses on Main Street in Edgartown - except for the small sign in front of the building. Built in 1873 in Edgartown, thousands of island tourists walk by the building each summer and hardly take notice of it. Jake Dellahunt parked his 1992 Ford F-150 4x4 in front of the building, stepped out of the truck and entered.

Jake had called ahead and sat at one end of a table in a small windowless conference room located on the first floor. Jake waited a few minutes until a deputy sheriff ushered in an inmate dressed in orange jailhouse coveralls. Jake quickly recognized Anderson from the booking pictures in the newspapers.

"Can you give us a few moments, deputy?" Jake asked and the deputy sheriff walked out. "I'll be right outside if you need me, Mr. Dellahunt."

After Jake introduced himself, the two men sat at opposite ends of the table. Jake studied Anderson and took his measure without saying a word. He was a small, frail, balding man in his early sixties, perhaps thirty years older than Jake. Jake could see the strained expression on his weather-beaten face. Anderson folded his boney hands on the table as if in prayer and Jake could see them trembling. Jake got up and sat next to Anderson.

"I thought I had seen most of the all-year-round people on the island, but I don't think I've ever seen you before, Mr. Anderson."

"Don't get out much, Mistuh Dellahunt. Just drive to church on Sundays and to the Up-Island Market for food Wednesdays."

"You're a church going man?"

"Have to be. Am Deacon of the Congregational Church in Chilmahk."

"I want you to start at the beginning and tell me what you know about killing this dog."

Anderson lowered his eyes and looked straight ahead as if in a hypnotic trance. The expression on his face changed to a solemn asceticism. "I don't know nuthin' about killin' no dog. Shuah, I had some words with the family about my chickens, but I don't know nuthin' about killin' a dog and doing that other stuff."

"What 'words' did you have with the family?"

"I've been chasing their black dog out of my chicken coops for a couple a months off and on. He'd get to digging under the wire 'n kill a few chickens. When I'd hear the ruckus, I'd come out of the house with my 12 gauge and fire it in the air. Mind yah, jest to scare him ahff. You got to believe me, Mistuh Dellahunt. I didn't kill that there dog."

Jake could see tears forming in the old man's eyes. "When did you talk to the dog owners?"

"Each time their dog'd kill my stock, I'd talk to them. Pretty nigh every week for two months. They promised they'd chain the dog up, but the kid let him off the chain 'n he'd come right back and kill more of my chickens."

"Did you ever threaten to kill the dog?"

"I was pretty mad at that family and might a said somethin' like that."

Jake got up.

"Do you believe me, Mistah Dellahunt?"

Jake thought a minute. "It's not important I believe you. It's important a jury believes you."

"It's important to know you believe in me. You're my lawyah. Ain't yah?"

Jake dodged a response. "I'm going to ask for a change of venue."

"What's that?" Anderson asked.

"I want the case moved to Boston."

"No. I'm against that," Anderson fired back quickly. "I'm not going to the city. Rather go to hell than breathe in that there poisoned air."

Jake knew islanders were told from birth the pollution in the air in the city would kill them, despite the millions who lived there proving the very opposite. Jake didn't dwell on the islander's agoraphobia. It was more important to explain the reasons he wanted the case off-island. "Look, they shoot people in Boston almost every day. There's hundreds of murder cases each year in the city. They have lots of serious crimes. Do you think the court wants to waste its time on some dog shooting case when the dockets are choked up with murder cases? They'll give you a slap on the wrist for shooting a dog that was killing your chickens. With all the newspaper stories around here, you'll never get a fair trial on the Vineyard. In Boston, this won't make a half paragraph on page 20 in the Boston Herald."

Anderson gritted his teeth and dug in his heels. "I didn't shoot that there dog and I'm not leaving Martha's Vineyard."

"Why not?" Jake asked.

"If the truth be told, I haven't been off this island in forty years and I'm not steppin' on any ferry now. I was born here and here I'm stayin'."

Jake could see further discussion for the moment was useless. "Fair enough. One last question, Mr. Anderson. I'm curious. You could have sold your land for a lot of money. Why didn't you?"

"That land's been in my family for over a hundred years. I'm not sellin' my land to a pack of vultures to build a bunch of condos in Chilmark and that's the end of it."

Jake moved toward the door. "There's a bail hearing this afternoon. I'll see you in court," Jake said and then knocked on the door for the deputy.

*

Jake called Skeeter on his cell phone and told him he would be a few minutes late. When Jake parked his truck next to Frank's Island Café and Donut Shop, Skeeter McLain was waiting for him on the deck.

The part-time island prosecutor sat dressed in his signature green pants, a blue blazer and a yacht club striped tie and blue dress shirt. "I'm asking the Judge to deny bail in the case, Jake. I want your guy to rot in jail. This is more than a simple animal cruelty case. It's attempted murder," the island prosecutor said and smiled at Jake.

Jake shook his head. "Maybe you can explain just how killing a dog turns into an attempted murder. Who was the victim, Lassie?"

"There was bad blood between Anderson and the family that owned the dog. He threatened them. When your client stuffed that dog's head in a mailbox, he knew the effect it would have on anyone in the family who opened the mailbox. It was a calculated act that showed a willful and depraved indifference to human life. In Massachusetts, that's second degree murder."

"Only if someone dies. Tell me who died."

"Nobody. That's why we're charging Anderson with an attempted manslaughter. The act was intended to deal a mortal blow to a family member."

"Really? The family member of a dog?"

"Yes."

"You check the law on this one, Skeeter?"

"Don't have to."

Jake reached in his pocket and pulled out an envelope. "Here are photocopies of my motions for the release of Mr. Anderson on his personal recognizance and a motion to dismiss the aggravated assault counts and dismiss the attempted murder charge." Jake stood up. "See you at the 2:00 P.M. Motion Session, Skeeter."

Skeeter looked at the pieces of paper. "They're not even typed. They're hand written."

"My secretary, Penny had the day off. Didn't have time this morning to type it," Jake shouted half way down the street. "Don't worry. Judge Graham will accept it."

Jake left his pickup in front of Frank's place and walked back to his office, first stopping at the Grapes of Wrath Bookstore to ask the two women who worked in the store to gather some material for him and drop it off upstairs right after lunch. He went up to his offices and picked up two books from his law library and then headed back to his house on Lake Tashmoo for lunch.

Jake Dellahunt never quite understood why few people ever locked their doors on the island. When Jake first arrived on the island he had asked about this fascinating custom of leaving your house wide open to be robbed blind. He was told few serious crimes are ever committed on the island because escape was impossible. Nobody could leave the island once the ferry service had been shut down, the airport closed and the two coast guard stations were put on alert.

Jake never accepted the theory escape from the island was impossible or crimes always would be discovered before the culprits fled the island. He was a city boy and he never put much stock in leaving his house unlocked. And so he found it both disconcerting and pleasantly surprising to take out his keys and unlock his front door only to discover the door was unlocked and to find his ex-wife, Maggie sitting in the living room.

She stood up, waiving her old house key in the air. As she rose, the long fur coat draped over her shoulders fell to the floor. He could not take his eyes off her. She was poured into a pair of jeans that hugged her body like a fresh coat of paint. She was as luscious and beautiful as a flower opening in the sunlight.

Her voice was pure velvet. "Hello Jake," she purred. "It's been a long time."

"I never stopped thinking about you," he replied and slowly walked to her. He picked her up in his arms and kissed her long and hard. She threw her arms around his neck so tightly he could hardly breathe. Her passion surprised him and Jake realized how much he had missed her. Glued to each other, she fell on top of him onto the divan. He felt his heart racing as he kissed her. It had been such a very long time. Afterwards, he held her close until he had to leave for court.

*

Jake Dellahunt walked into court that afternoon with a smile on his face.

"You look pretty chipper today counsel," quipped the clerk of the Superior Court as Jake took his seat at the defense table next to his client. He said nothing to his client, John Anderson, who had shaved and changed into his Sunday best his wife had brought him. Jake set the two law books he carried with him on the table and then he pulled out of his briefcase a dozen or more Vineyard Times and Vineyard Gazette newspapers the two women from the Grapes of Wrath Bookstore had left for him in his office.

He glanced to his right and saw the part-time Assistant District Attorney, Skeeter McLain adorned in his customary pair of green pants, sitting next to Alfred Norton, the Dukes County district attorney. Except for lawyers arguing motions, few people ever showed up at these sessions. Jake knew killing and mutilating a dog on the island would be a high profile case. Still, he was surprised at the number of spectators who filled the small courtroom and gallery. Norton rarely appeared in a courtroom and Jake thought it unusual to find the Dukes County district attorney sitting beside Skeeter at the prosecutor's table. As he glanced backward, he saw Maggie as beautiful as ever, standing in the back of the courtroom.

Judge Graham walked in and stood behind the bench. She was an imposing figure in her long, black judicial robes, gray hair coiffed carefully and looking very much like the picture of Lady Justice. Judges on the Superior Court travel the circuit and she had rotated from three months on the bench in the Berkshires to sit in the spring session on Martha's Vineyard. Jake had tried a handful of cases against her in Boston when she was an assistant U. S. Attorney and he knew she had a summer house on the island in Oak Bluffs. He also was aware she had two black Labrador Retrievers she adored.

Everyone stood while the bailiff called out, *"Hear ye, hear ye, hear ye, please rise. All persons having anything to do before the Dukes County Superior Court, the justice of this court draw near, give your attention and you shall be heard. God save the Commonwealth of Massachusetts and this honorable court."*

The judge glanced at Jake momentarily. Then she took in the crowded courtroom and turned to the clerk puzzled by the large number of spectators who overflowed the courtroom. "Isn't this the motion session?" she asked her clerk of court.

"Yes, Your Honor. There is only one matter before you this afternoon, "Defendant's Motions to Dismiss All Counts of an

Attempted Murder, Dismissal of All Counts of Assault and Trespass and a Motion to Grant Bail."

No matter how many times before he had traveled this route, Jake's heart started pounding when the case was called. *"Docket Number 121305, Commonwealth vs. John Anderson. Are all parties present and ready?"*

Both Jake and Skeeter stood and responded affirmatively and the clerk placed Jake's handwritten motions in front of the Judge. Jake waited still standing.

"Mr. Dellahunt, these motions are handwritten. The rule is clear all submissions to the court must be typed on paper or sent as electronic transmissions," she said.

Jake rose to his feet. "Yes, Your Honor. I was called by Mr. Anderson a few hours ago from the Edgartown jail and did not have time to type the motions. Our internet service is down on the island which is not unusual. I will present this court with duplicate motions in proper form in the morning. May I proceed?" Jake asked.

The judge nodded and Jake continued. "I was told by the bail commissioner the district attorney is seeking to deny bail and I was hoping your honor would consider the substance of the motions rather than the form of the paperwork. I submit justice will be better served to set a reasonable bail and allow this elderly defendant to avoid spending any more time in the jail." Jake finished and held his breath.

"Attempted murder and mutilating a dog. These are serious charges, Mr. Dellahunt."

"I agree, Your Honor. However, I believe there is a credible defense to all these charges."

Judge Graham nodded her head. "Alright, Mr. Dellahunt, just be sure to give the clerk typed copies tomorrow."

Skeeter McLain jumped up. "I object, Your Honor. These motions are required to be typewritten."

"Did Mr. Dellahunt give you a copy of them?"

"Yes."

"Then sit down. I've made my ruling."

"One other thing, Judge," Jake continued. "I would request an evidentiary hearing on these motions. I would like the court to swear in two witnesses, take judicial notice of several documents and hear testimony bearing on these motions."

"Which motions in particular do you want me to hear evidence?"

"The motions to dismiss all counts of attempted murder, assault and trespass."

"And the motion to grant bail?"

"We can dispose of that without an evidentiary hearing your honor."

"Then let's go forward on the issue of bail. I will hear from the government solely on the defendant's motion to grant bail," The judge ordered and nodded to Mr. Greenpants to begin.

Skeeter McLain stood and cleared his throat. Taking photos of the dog's severed head from his briefcase, he placed them on the table in plain view of the judge, which was a cheap shot and clearly against the rules of court. "This is one of the most heinous cases we have ever encountered on the island of Martha's Vineyard. Defendant shot a neighbor's dog, decapitated the animal and then placed the dog's head in the neighbor's mailbox."

McLain looked over to the defense table and pointed to the defendant. "The defendant threatened to kill the dog. When Mr. Anderson stuffed that dog's head in a mailbox, he knew the effect it would have on anyone in the family who opened the mailbox. It was a calculated act that showed a willful and depraved indifference to human life. In Massachusetts, that's second degree murder. The act was designed to kill or attempt to kill. It constituted an attempted second degree murder."

"Save the rhetoric and the photos you've placed on the table for trial, Mr. McLain," Judge Graham admonished. "Are the counts for attempted murder in the second degree the only reason the government is opposing granting bail? Let me be clear. Are you opposing bail because of an attempted manslaughter?"

"Yes."

"Who was the victim?"

"The person who discovered the dog's head in the mailbox."

"But nobody came close to dying except for a dog and I've never heard of anyone being charged with attempted manslaughter. Do you have any cases supporting your legal theories?"

"I do." Skeeter handed copies of the cases to the clerk to give to the judge.

Judge Graham read the cases quickly and looked at the prosecution table. "These purport to be two California cases on attempted manslaughter where the California court accepted the theory of an attempted manslaughter. We are not bound in Massachusetts by decisions of other states," she pointed out. "Did you find any cases in Massachusetts?"

"No, Your Honor, but the cases in California do support the validity of attempted manslaughter as a proper charge."

The judge turned to Jake. "What do you have to say, Mr. Dellahunt?"

Jake held up the two law books. "Since the reason the government is refusing bail is based on the counts related to attempted second degree murder or attempted manslaughter, I found the Restatement of Criminal Law in Massachusetts and the leading case dispositive on this issue. May I give them to the clerk for Your Honor to review?"

Judge Graham nodded. She scanned the cases Jake had marked. After a few minutes, she turned to Jake and said, "From the materials submitted, I am not reasonably convinced the charge of attempted manslaughter exists or does not exist in our Massachusetts Law. I will hold the issue under advisement until I have had a chance to review the law. For the moment, Mr. Dellahunt, I will not dismiss the charges of attempted murder in the second degree."

Jake remained standing, poker faced and disappointed. "Will Your Honor allow me to speak to the matter of bail?"

"Don't interrupt me, Mr. Dellahunt," the Judge chided. "I was about to say I believe nobody was killed in the case, except of course for a dog. I am therefore disposed to hearing arguments on granting bail. All other motions in the case will be heard at ten o'clock tomorrow morning."

The clerk stood up and repeated the Judge's orders continuing all the motions except for the issue of bail until the next morning.

*

After Jake portrayed Mr. Anderson as agoraphobic, not leaving the island for forty years because of a fear of breathing the poisoned air on the mainland, Judge Graham released Mr. Anderson on his personal recognizance. Downstairs in the court foyer, the *Vineyard Gazette, Times and WCIB, Cape and Islands Broadcasting*, interviewed Jake and then the reporters left. Jake looked out one of the windows for Maggie, but only saw an angry crowd gathering outside, parading around the courthouse with signs hanging Anderson in effigy. He left through a back door, hustled Mr. and Mrs. Anderson into his pickup and quickly took off while the crowds watched them leave with hatred in their eyes.

After a few minutes of silence, John Anderson spoke. "Want to thank yah for getting' me out of jail, Mistah Dellahunt. Yah certainly sounded fine, but I'm not so sure we won or lost."

Jake looked over to him as they drove along State Road. "I think it was a tie. We'll know more tomorrow when we return."

"Thank yah, anyhow, Mistah Dellahunt."

"You're welcome. Please call me Jake. Just one other thing today. Which bank would you like to go to?"

"No bank. Don't trust no banks, Mistah Dellahunt. Got the money all safe and sound at my house. You take cash, don't yah?"

*

After making a deposit in the old stone bank on Main Street in Vineyard Haven, Jake drove directly home. Maggie's suitcase was gone and he found a note on the coffee table in the living room. He read it over and over and then walked to the cabinet and pulled out a bottle of Dewar's. Just then, there was a tap at the window and Jake looked up. A big Wampanoag Indian, framed by the window, admonished him with his beefy index finger. The former Chief of the Wampanoag Tribal Council, Robert Paul, was Jake's best friend and handyman. There wasn't much they didn't know about one another. Jake walked out onto the deck and handed the note to the big Indian without a word. He read the note aloud: "Dear Jake, Sorry, but I went back to Los Angeles. I think it best. I didn't get the chance to thank you for agreeing to take the two boys for the summer. They loved the island and dream about returning. I want them to know their father. Thanks and good luck with your murder case. Maggie."

Jake finished off the rest of the scotch in the glass. He sat on the rocker and poured another couple of slugs out of the bottle.

Robert Paul was plainly vexed. "I heard she was on the island this morning. I'm sorry she left, but if you have one more drink out of that bottle, I'm going to say something I shouldn't. Oh, hell, I'm going to say it anyways. It was the damned booze that got you into this mess in the first place. So why the hell are you starting again?"

"How long we known each other, chief?"

"I been your handyman, cook and house sitter for ten years. Before that for Judge Sam, when he was alive."

"And we've been friends for as long as I can remember. Maggie and me and the kids had a life here."

"It was the best for all of us, Jake."

"Yeah, it was great. So what happened?"

"You know exactly what happened. She had enough of your damned drinking and you got hooked up with the wrong people and some bimbo in Oak Bluffs."

"She took the kids with her to California five years ago. She won't let me see them."

"Do you blame her?"

He read the note again. He walked back inside and put the bottle back in the cabinet and wondered why she really came three thousand miles to the island. Jake sat on the divan for a long time, thinking about Maggie and the two boys.

It had been a long day. He glanced at the flashing light on his answering machine and recognized the number on the display. It was his paralegal, Penny Pacheco. News travels fast on the island. He hit the "play messages" button. She wanted to know if Jake needed her to come into the office to help on the Anderson matter. Penny was born and bred on the island. If anyone knew the answers to Jake's lingering questions about John Anderson, she would. And Jake still had a few unanswered questions.

*

The Edgartown courthouse is an ample two-story colonial building on Main Street with four white pillars prominently set flush against the red brick exterior. Two symmetrical, double-storied, brick wings on either side of the central building extend sideways and lend the structure a spacious appearance.

Jake arrived at the courthouse well before the first call of the list. By the time he drove up, The Audubon Society, the All-Island Animal Rights Groups, and the Society for Prevention of Cruelty to Animals had already gathered on the sidewalk in front of the building behind a row of wooden horses. They marched in a wide circle, holding up their signs and placards vilifying John Anderson as they chanted over and over, "Ho, Ho, Don't Let Him Go. Take his head; like he did." A dozen island policemen kept the entrance and walkway clear.

Jake decided to take the side door to avoid the mob. He climbed the stairs to the second floor conference room. He closed the door and set his briefcase down on the conference table. A few minutes later, the door opened and the Andersons entered. Before they took seats, Jake turned to Mrs. Anderson and asked her to meet them in the courtroom. "I am sorry. But I'm going to have to ask you to leave."

"She's a part of this, Mistah Dellahunt. She can stay, if she wants."

"No she can't, Mr. Anderson. Anything you tell me is privileged so long as there's nobody else listening."

"Even my wife of forty years."

"Yes."

She quickly turned without a word and left the room.

Jake turned back to Anderson. "I am sorry about that. Did you have any trouble getting into the courthouse this morning?"

"That was considerable easier than the trouble last night," Anderson said.

"What happened last night?"

"Some son-of-bitch tried tah burn my house down around midnight."

"Did you see who did it?"

"Me and my misses were pretty busy puttin' out the fire. She smelled the smoke and woke me. I run out and thought I saw a small pickup truck pulling out of our dirt road. Too dark to tell yah the color or make. I took out the garden hoses and the Misses called the Chilmark Police and Volunteer Fire Department."

"Who do you think did such a thing?"

"I dunno. The whole island is pretty riled up right now. We're so scared we're thinking about moving away when the trial is all over."

Jake checked his watch. "This morning, we're going to try to nip these charges in the bud in the motion session. If it works, we'll only have to deal with one count of animal cruelty. If it works well, maybe you'll walk out a free man."

They talked for a while until it was nearly ten. "Look, I'm going to answer the first call of the motion list and will be back in about ten minutes. Stay here and keep the door locked until I get back."

"No need to worry none about me, Mistah Dellahunt. I kin take care of myself."

Jake rose and headed for the door. "There's a lot of people who want to see you in jail or worse, John. You're paying a lot of money for my counsel. Take it and stay put."

*

"All right Mr. Dellahunt, you may call your first witness."

"Call the Defendant, John Anderson."

Anderson rose from the defense table, entered the witness box and was sworn in.

Jake walked over to his client. "Just have three questions for you Mr. Anderson. First, did you shoot your neighbor's dog and then put the head of the animal in your neighbor's mailbox?"

"No, sir. I'd nevah do such a thing."

"Second, were you recently offered thirty million dollars to sell your farm in Chilmark?"

Anderson was not prepared for the question. He hesitated and then said, "I'd rather not say."

Jake returned to the defense table and pulled the copies of the *Vineyard Gazette and Times* from his briefcase. He held them up to the Judge. "I would ask the Court to take judicial notice of the stories about an offer to buy Mr. Anderson's real estate in these local island newspapers."

Skeeter jumped to his feet. "Objection, Your Honor. Newspapers are inadmissible under the best evidence rule. Let Mr. Dellahunt put in direct evidence of the offer, if there ever was an offer."

The judge turned to Skeeter. "This is not a trial, Mr. McLain. It's just a motion session. I am not bound by the strict rules of evidence to support motions to dismiss. However, I am going to instruct the witness to answer the question. Please repeat your question, Mr. Dellahunt."

"Again, Mr. Anderson, were you offered thirty million dollars to sell your property in Chilmark?"

"Yes sir, I was."

"And lastly, can you tell the court who made the offer?"

"I got the offer in the mail from an outfit called, the Bahston Investment Group. I called the number in the letter in Bahston. Told them I'd never sell to anyone who'd turn the land into condominiums. This is Martha's Vineyard, I told them. Land is sacred here."

"Those were your exact words? 'You'd never sell.'"

"My exact words."

Jake sat down and said, "You may inquire, Mr. District Attorney."

Skeeter rose from his chair and stood smiling, like he had just been handed a winning lottery ticket. "Like Mr. Dellahunt," he began, "I only have three questions. The dog was killed with a shotgun. My first question is do you own a shotgun, Mr. Anderson?"

"Yes, a twelve gauge."

"Secondly, did you threaten to shoot the dog?"

"Might have said somethin' like that to them."

"I'll take that for a yes, Mr. Anderson," McLain said and waited to be contradicted, but Anderson just looked straight ahead and said nothing more.

"And lastly, did you ever fire your shotgun while the dog was on your property?"

"That dog was killing my chickens, mistah."

"Just a simple yes or no. Did you shoot your gun when the dog was on your property?"

"Yes, but. . ."

"That's all. I have nothing more your honor."

"You may step down, Mr. Anderson," the judge said. "Call your next witness, Mr. Dellahunt." Anderson left the witness box and returned to the defense table.

"Call Skeeter McLain."

McLain was instantly incensed. Without thinking, he flailed his arms at the defense table and looked directly at Jake with a smirk on his face. "You can't call me," he shouted. "I'm the goddamned prosecutor in this case."

Judge Graham banged her gavel on the bench. "Mr. McLain, you will direct your comments to me. Do you understand?"

Skeeter looked up at the bench. He collected himself as best he could and quickly blurted out,

"Sorry Your Honor. Please note my strong objection to being called as a witness."

The judge turned to Jake. "What in the world are you doing, Mr. Dellahunt? You're asking the district attorney's office to testify in a criminal proceeding?"

"I am Your Honor, but just for the purposes of the motions to dismiss. I would ask the court for some latitude to inquire into a possible conflict of interest."

Alfred Norton, the Dukes County district attorney was sitting at the prosecution table. He stood up. "I would like to be heard on this matter of calling my assistant district attorney to the stand."

"Sit down, Al. I'm running this session," Judge Graham had her hackles up. "Mr. Dellahunt has the right to call any witness he likes. And I am going to allow him to call McLain to the stand. Swear in the witness, Mr. Clerk."

Jake rose to his feet and stood at the defense table. "Mr. McLain, you're the part-time Assistant District Attorney on the island. What does that mean?"

"It means I can practice law, but not in criminal matters."

"For example, you can and do represent insurance companies defending accident cases?"

"Yes, I represent several insurance companies."

"And you appear in the Probate Court for estate matters?"

"Yes, I am allowed under special rules in Dukes County."

Al Norton rose to his feet, "Judge, what relevance does Mr. McLain's work have to motions to dismiss in this matter?"

"I'm wondering the same thing," Judge Graham said and turned toward Jake. "Get to the point, counselor."

"Yes, Your Honor. Mr. McLain, do you also represent clients buying and selling real estate on the island?"

"Yes, some."

"Is that your answer, 'some?' Isn't it a substantial part of your income?"

"Depends on what you mean by 'substantial.'"

"Fair enough. Ever represent an outfit called the Boston Investment Group?"

"I can't remember every client I've represented, Mr. Dellahunt," Skeeter said smugly.

"Weren't you in the courtroom when Mr. Anderson testified he received a thirty million dollar offer from the Boston Investment Group to buy his farm and he said he'd never sell the land?"

"I remember."

Jake pulled a blank yellow legal pad of paper from his briefcase and looked at it for a minute as if reading something on the page. He carefully held the pad so that Skeeter could not see there was nothing written on it.

"I'm going to ask you once again, Mr. McLain. Did you ever represent the Boston Investment Group?"

Skeeter looked at the legal pad Jake held in his hand. "What have you got in your hand? Show it to me."

Jake knew he had him. "I'm asking the questions here. Did you ever represent the Boston Investment Group?"

"I don't recall."

Just then the courtroom door opened and Jake's paralegal, Penny Pacheco walked into the courtroom and moved to the railing behind the defense table. She held up several documents and handed them to Jake. He read the first page quickly.

Jake approached the witness and placed the first document on the edge of witness box. "Does this refresh your recollection? It's a certified fax of the papers the Boston Investment Group filed at the Secretary of State's Office in Boston. Isn't that your name and address on the document naming you as the principal officer, director and clerk? "

Skeeter said nothing.

Jake pulled out the next three sheets. "Did you notify by email The Audubon Society, the All-Island Animal Rights Groups, and the Society for Prevention of Cruelty to Animals that Mr. Anderson killed a dog and mutilated it and he would be in court today?"

"So what? There's nothing wrong with that."

"And where were you last night about midnight?"

Jake could see he hit a nerve. Jake held up the last document Penny had handed him. It was a picture of Skeeter's small red pickup truck with a close-up of white chicken droppings still stuck to a front tire.

"You were a partner in the Boston Investment Group. You wanted Anderson off the island and knew he would never leave unless you forced him to sell out. You killed that dog, Skeeter. When you severed the dog's head and placed it in the owner's mailbox, you made it impossible for Mr. Anderson to remain on the island. When you knew he was going to fight back in court, you tried to burn him out of his house. It was about the money, wasn't it?"

Skeeter looked pathetic. Unable to answer, he folded like a card table.

Judge Graham advised Skeeter of rights against self-incrimination and the bailiff led him away. Dukes County District Attorney, Al Norton rose to his feet and asked for a dismissal of all charges against John Anderson and Judge Graham ordered the charges dismissed.

*

The next morning, Frank Falcone was having coffee with his early morning regulars when he spotted Jake at the counter inside the café and donut shop. He motioned Jake over to an empty inside table.

"I hear congratulations are in order. You did a hell of a job for the chicken farmer yesterday. It didn't take you long to win."

"Good for him, bad for me. I'm going to have to give him back most of his retainer. The case didn't get far."

"Maybe you can earn it back. I hear Skeeter's looking for counsel. Would you take his case?"

"Only if he buys different color pants."

"With all the excitement on the island the last few days, I was wondering if you had a chance to call the Massachusetts Department of Public Utilities?" Frank queried.

"As a matter of fact, I've meaning to talk to you about that very matter."

"So you did reach them."

"In a manner of speaking," Jake responded cautiously.

"And . . ."

"And I want your solemn promise you'll never ever again ask me to pay you anything on the accident case you sent over. Never."

"OK, OK. Don't get riled up. Spill it. What happened?"

"Do you know why Massachusetts Department of Public Utilities sent you that letter?"

"Cause I hacked them off for ten thousand dollars of free electricity. That's a no-brainer."

"No, Mass DPU sent you that letter because Cape and Islands Power Company filed a complaint with the DPU. The DPU was collecting for the power company."

"Like a collection agency."

"You're exactly right. So I spoke to Cape and Island's general counsel after court yesterday and he agreed to drop all the charges and wipe your slate clean."

"What's that mean, Jake?"

"You walk away paying nothing."

"I pay nothing? Come on, what's the catch?"

"Nothing. Absolutely nothing."

"Really? How did you manage that Jake?"

"Does David Copperfield tell his secrets? Does Macy tell Gimbals? Me tell you?"

"How about free donuts for life?"

"Don't tempt me. OK. Remember telling me you were paying a monthly kickback to the guy who approached you in order to lower your electric bills. Did you know he's a meter reader for the Cape and Islands Power Company?"

Frank was puzzled. He looked at Jake. "So what?"

Jake shook his head. It was all so easy to put together. "Don't you get it? He works for the power company and he's been taking kickbacks from you and other customers all over the island to stick a bunch of magnets on the meters and lower energy bills."

"OK." Frank still didn't get it.

"You were just one of a dozen or more unlucky customers who got caught. Everyone else settled by paying without admitting any guilt. So far, the power company hadn't figured out there's only one person putting magnets on the meters."

Frank's eyes lit up. "And they wanted to know his name."

"Bingo. And you gave it to me, Frank. I made the trade, his name for your clean slate."

"And what happens if I gave you the wrong guy's name? Not that I'm saying I gave you the wrong name. Just what would happen?"

"What would happen, Frank? Get your will in order because one of these days, I'm going to kill you."

Chapter Three
The Case of the Proxigean Tide

The Blues had been running all week off Lambert's Cove. The big Indian sat at the center console and throttled back the Mercury Black Max 200 outboard engine hanging off the Mako 22's stern, while Jake tied an umbrella lure to the end of a wire leader. As the boat settled down to trolling speed, Jake played out a couple hundred feet of line, then hit the drag on the reel, setting the rod into a holder on the gunwale. Jake looked out at the trailing wake and considered this was the first time he had gone fishing without his sons.

Jake turned and shouted to the Wampanoag Indian holding the wheel, "Let's run up the shoals for a while, Chief. Just keep an eye on her depth finder and fuel gauge. Don't want to run aground or out of gas."

Robert Paul sat at the controls and shook his head. "Jake, I bathed in these shoals before you learned to walk. And don't be worrying about how much fuel we have; worry about paying for the gas when your credit card bill comes this month."

77

Jake watched the lines running along the shallows where frenzied Blues churned the water into white foam, chasing baitfish that jumped into the air trying to escape being shredded alive by needle-sharp teeth. As the lure passed through the shoaling water, one Bluefish hit the umbrella rig and ran deep. The line zinged out and Jake grabbed the rod, set the hook and adjusted the drag while Robert Paul eased the engine into neutral. Jake felt the line grow taut as the fish struggled to free itself in deeper water and the light fiberglass rod bowed like a piece of wet spaghetti. Suddenly, the fish broke the surface and tried to spit the lure out of its mouth.

Then the line ran out again and Jake felt the rush of excitement. "You see that, Chief? He's one big son-of-a-bitch – maybe twenty pounds."

"You better pull that fish in quick, because there be company coming," Robert Paul shouted and pointed to the 250 foot Martha's Vineyard Steamship Authority's ferry boat running at full tilt outside of the channel and toward them.

Jake looked up. "It's the freight boat." He started reeling in.

The Indian stood up and raised his outstretched hand onto his forehead, shading his eyes from the morning sun. Looking like Dallin's Indian Scout on the Plains, he shouted, "It's the *Katama*, and she's bearing passengers. I do not think they see us."

Jake kept reeling in line. "If it keeps coming, it's going to ground on the shoals and roll right over us." Jake stopped reeling in. He put the rod back in the holder, picked up a knife in the tackle box and shouted, "I hate to do this." Then he cut the line. "Let's get the hell out of its way, Chief – and fast."

*

The next morning, Jake sat on the outside deck of Frank's Island Café and Donut Shop sipping his early morning Joe and bent over the local newspapers. The *Vineyard Gazette* and the *Vineyard Times* had published special editions with a banner headline under their mastheads: "87 PASSENGERS INJURED IN ISLAND FERRY MISHAP." He carefully perused the story about the Coast Guard evacuating passengers from the grounded ferry, *Katama,* and "the former Boston lawyer and prominent island attorney, Jake Dellahunt, had witnessed the grounding from his Mako fishing boat along with retired Wampanoag Tribal Council Chief, Robert Paul. Mr. Dellahunt said he didn't know how the accident could have happened without someone being asleep at the switch, and he thought the passengers had a good legal case against the Steamship Authority for negligence. Mr. Dellahunt and Mr. Paul helped transport several seriously injured passengers to the Vineyard Hospital in Oak Bluffs."

Jake searched for a reason why the ferry ran aground, but there was none in either newspaper. Jake put the papers down and picked up his mug of coffee.

"I saw the newspapers this morning. You're a hero, Mr. Jake Dellahunt."

Jake looked up to see an attractive black woman dressed in hospital whites, holding a large Styrofoam cup of coffee in her hand. He recognized her right away and motioned her to sit across from him.

"Just for a moment," she said and carefully pulled off the tab on the cover of her coffee cup. She was the emergency room admitting doctor who had treated passengers Jake had brought to the hospital. The name tag pinned on her white jacket read: "Josephine Hayes, MD."

Jake guessed she was fifteen years younger than he was and he noticed she wasn't wearing a wedding band on her finger. He also noticed the two engaging dimples that broke out on her cheeks every time she smiled.

"You did a fine job yesterday. Are you headed back to the hospital, Dr. Hayes?" Jake asked.

"Actually I'm just getting off work. Going home to catch a few Z's."

"How are the passengers?"

"When the ferry ran aground yesterday, the passengers were thrown forward. Some suffered broken bones and concussions. We only lost one person. He was thrown off the ferry and he probably severed his cervical vertebrae in the fall."

Dr. Hayes looked at him intently while Jake mulled over the information. She finally asked,

"What are you thinking about?"

Jake wasn't going to admit his brain was hard wired to a courtroom and he was thinking about the death case against the Steamship Authority. "I am truly sorry to hear someone died. I was wondering if he suffered."

"I don't think he had time. The fall killed him."

Pity, Jake thought. It would be a much better case if the guy hadn't died all that fast. Lingering on death's doorway paid a hell of a lot better than instant death. He looked up at her and politely replied, "That's too bad."

"That he died or he died without conscious pain and suffering?" she quipped.

He laughed at her. "Are you always that cynical?"

"Well, counselor, wasn't that going through your mind?"

"Doctor and mind reader, too. And a cynical mind reader at that."

"When it comes to lawyers, I am."

"Not all lawyers, I hope. Was he from the island?"

"His name was Mayhew. Arthur Mayhew. Did you know him?"

"I'm sorry to say I didn't." Jake took a sip of coffee. He thought about how the long winter had whittled down his meager caseload. He made a mental note to go to the funeral, offer his condolences and slip the wife his business card with the standard offer: "… if I can be of any help." Jake saw no shame in taking the dead man's case, even without conscious pain and suffering. The humiliation was in having to ask for it.

Jake quickly changed the subject. "You attached, Dr. Hayes?"

"Only to the practice of medicine, and please call me Jo. What about you, Mr. Dellahunt? Married with children?"

"It's Jake. I'm divorced and have two sons, nine and fourteen. They live in Los Angeles with my ex-wife."

"Maggie Dellahunt, the movie actress?"

"Yep, the one and only. May I call you, Jo? I mean, may I call you on the phone?" Then Jake thought aloud. "You go out with white guys, don't you, Jo?" He was sorry the moment he said it.

She looked at him and smiled evocatively, as if someone she cared for once had asked her the same question. "Sure. You are kind of cute, you know. Let me have your cell phone."

Jake handed his phone to her and she dialed her cell number into his phone. "Now you've got my number. I'm on loan from Mass General for only three months, so don't wait too long. By the way, I gave his wife your name. I think she's going to call you or come in and see you."

"Who?"

"Mrs. Mayhew. She might have a case – a wrongful death case for her husband. That's what you were thinking about, wasn't it, counselor?"

Before Jake could answer, his cell phone rang and he opened it. Dr. Josephine Hayes got up and slipped away.

*

The call was from Jake's paralegal, Penny Pacheco. When she went to work that morning, she turned the corner at the Grapes of Wrath Bookstore and found a line of people, some in casts, others on crutches and in bandages, sitting on the stairs waiting to see "the prominent island attorney, Jake Dellahunt." They had read what he said in the morning's newspapers. She sat some of them in the waiting room, put others in the library, and stuffed the rest in the conference room. Then she called him on his cell phone. When Jake arrived at the office fifteen minutes later, a dozen more people sat on the stairs waiting to be shoehorned inside.

Jake recognized many of the ferry passengers from the accident and he triaged the new clients. He interviewed passengers in casts with fractures first, then those on crutches and others in bandages, while Penny collected information from passengers with less obvious soft tissue injuries. They worked through lunch collecting information. By late afternoon, Jake Dellahunt set an all-island record for signing up new personal injury cases in one day. Jake counted fifty-one passengers who had put their signatures on contingent fee agreements, hiring him to represent them for their injuries, big and small, including one death claim brought by Mrs. Alice Mayhew.

Jake and Penny were both bone tired when they closed the office. They walked slowly down the stairs. Penny stopped, shook her head and threw her hands in the air as if she had reached the end of her rope. "Jake, how in God's name are we going to handle all these cases? I mean, we're just a small law office. There's just the two of us."

"That doesn't bother me as much as finding what we're going to hang our hat on."

"What do you mean?"

"In a personal injury case, we need to prove someone was negligent and negligence caused our clients' injuries before we can collect a cent. In these civil personal injury cases, we need to prove the Steamship Authority or someone who worked on the boat was negligent."

"That shouldn't be too hard. Boats just don't simply run aground."

"Really? Not one single person I interviewed today seemed to know what caused the accident. Maybe the ferry captain fell asleep. Maybe they were playing cards in the wheelhouse. Maybe they were negligent – maybe not."

"But you said in the newspaper ..."

"I know what I said. But if passengers were injured by an act of God, like a bolt of lightning shorted out the controls, or a whale pushed the boat out of the channel, or a fish net fouled the ship's rudder, then there's no case. And that's only half the problem I see right now."

"What's the other half?"

"A lawyer can't take a case to court if there's a reasonable expectation the attorney will testify in the case."

"So what?"

"Cheezus. I witnessed the whole thing."

"And lawyers can't take a case to court if they are going to be called to testify."

"I think you've got it."

*

It seemed to Jake half the island was on Lambert's Cove Beach the next morning to watch a pair of tug boats haul the *Katama* off the shoals at high tide. Jake stood in the mist among a circus of people, some just standing around, others playing ball or throwing sticks in the water for their dogs to retrieve from the cold morning surf. Everyone on the beach wore parkas or sweats, blue jeans and sneakers, except for two men, who were dressed in dark suits, shirts and ties, and walked along the sandy beach in laced, black shoes. They headed straight for Jake. If they weren't the Blues Brothers, they were cops.

"Jake Dellahunt? Are you Jake Dellahunt?" one of them asked as he placed a piece of paper in Jake's hand. I'm Federal Agent Thomas O'Rourke and this is Federal Agent Patrick Callahan. We're from the National Transportation Safety Board. This is a federal subpoena requiring you to appear and testify at a deposition. If you fail to appear, a federal judge in Boston will issue a warrant for your arrest and you will be jailed for contempt."

Jake looked at the federal subpoena in disbelief. "I know the drill. You're the investigators for the ferry accident and you want me to testify."

"Affirmative to all of the above."

"You know, I wasn't on that ferry when it went aground. I really can't tell you anything about the accident. Besides, that rust bucket was built seventy years ago," he pointed out. "Maybe it fell apart from old age."

"That's not what you told the newspapers. You said it was negligence. How do you know?"

"Hey, you can't believe everything you read in the newspapers."

Just then, Frank Falcone, a fast-talking, former native New Yorker and proud owner of Frank's Island Café and Donut Shop, walked over. Jake was always getting Frank out of jams. Frank obviously thought this was one time he might reciprocate. "Hey Jake, are these two clowns bothering you? Because if they're shakin' your tree, I can handle them."

"Frank, they're the federal officers investigating the ferry accident."

"I can handle them, Jake."

"Frank, stay out of this. They're the feds."

"Ha, I don't give a crap. To me, they're just a couple of annoying horseflies on the beach."

Jake whispered to Frank, "Yeah, they may be a pair of beach buzzards to you, but they can put a mountain of groceries on my kitchen table."

The two agents overheard the conversation. One of them moved closer to Jake. "You're not very smart for a lawyer who's supposed to be fairly intelligent." Then they both turned and began walking away, leaving Jake holding the deposition subpoena. "See you at the deposition, Mr. Dellahunt."

"Not if I can help it, you won't," Jake shot back at them.

Jake looked at Frank and shook his head. "Jeezus Frank, don't you know those two feds are going to be the judge and jury in my ferry case? If they find the Steamship Authority guilty of negligence, you can forward my mail to St. Kitts every winter and to the South of France in the summers."

Frank thought a moment. "I can convince them Jake. Honest, I can. Let me take a crack at them."

Jake looked at Frank. Jake knew the native New Yorker did not leave the city voluntarily. He had to leave if he wanted to keep breathing. "Thanks for the offer, but I'll pass."

"I wasn't going to do nothing to them. Honest, Jake. Maybe give them a talkin' to. Give 'em some free coffee and donuts. You know, try to be nice to them."

"Please Francis. Promise me you're not going to do anything nice."

"Okay, have it your way. But I think you're makin' a mistake."

"Promise?"

"Promise."

Jake stuffed the federal subpoena in his pocket and drove back to the office. He spent the rest of the day drafting a "Motion to Quash a Deposition Subpoena." He wrote he had nothing to add to the investigation and his testimony would jeopardize his ability to represent the passengers who had hired him. He knew it was a thin premise to pin his hopes on, but it was the truth. "Not that the truth matters much," he thought aloud when he'd finished writing. He pulled up a few case citations from Westlaw to support the argument and left the motion, affidavit, and "Memorandum in Support of a Motion to Quash" ready for Penny to file electronically in the morning. Then he locked up and headed home.

*

Spring was quickly turning to summer and the date Jake had circled in red on the kitchen calendar heralding the arrival of Jake's two sons was drawing close. There was a flurry of last-minute preparations. Robert Paul sent out the sails for repair while Jake and the big Indian moved the sailboat from the shed and tied it to the end of the dock on the other side of the Mako 22, with water skis, ample lines, extra life jackets, air horns and anchors at the ready. After Robert Paul promised Jake the boys would never take out a boat without the Indian tagging along, Jake rented a Kawasaki two-seater jet ski from Maciel's for the kids to tool around on Lake Tashmoo. The guest room was freshly painted and the twin beds were made up with new sheets and pillow cases.

Jake closed up the office early that Friday evening and drove home. He set his briefcase on the hall table and walked into the kitchen. Robert Paul, dressed in jeans, an old t-shirt and wearing a size 4 xtra-large grilling apron, stood in front of a stovetop, boiling water next to a pair of lobsters several feet long, nervously pacing back and forth on top of the kitchen counter. Jake moved closer to the counter to have a better look at them. "Chief, don't let those two monsters escape."

"I have them boxed in pretty good. Just keep your hands away from the claws of the big one. He is pretty pissed off right now and I do not like the way he looks at you."

Jake moved back a safe distance. "Where did you get them? From a traveling zoo?"

"I set traps last night on this side of the inlet. Our lobsters run big after a full moon. One is eight pounds and the other, the big one, about twelve."

Jake took off his jacket and loosened his tie. He pulled a soda out of the refrigerator and walked back to the counter to look at the size of the two crustaceans. "Do we eat them or is it the other way around?"

The big Wampanoag wrapped his huge hand around the back of the bigger one. As he lifted the creature in the air, it fought back furiously, whipping its tail up and down, and trying to get its claws turned around to take a piece of the Indian's hand. "Let me show you something, boss." He held the lobster up with one hand while he stroked its underbelly with his other. After a while, the lobster stopped moving. He laid it on its back on the counter and moved away from it. "It sleeps now. I will throw it in the pot of boiling water head first, so it will feel nothing."

"How did you do that? Make the lobster unconscious?"

"It is an old Indian trick. I can teach you."

"Not on that moose! When you trap its baby, I'll try it," Jake responded and walked into the living room to check the mail. "Did Bob Cottle finish the window screens?"

"They were over this morning and so was the plumber. The boys' shower works fine."

"We've been waiting three months for that plumber. Now he's going to wait three months to get paid."

"No boss, he said you being a lawyer and all, we had to pay before he would begin today. Says he don't trust no lawyers."

"That's a compliment coming from him. Where did you get the money to pay him?"

"It was the boat money. You know, cash for gasoline we keep in the kitchen drawer."

"We call him every day and he doesn't come for three months. He shows up and gets paid for the job before he even starts. I should have been a plumber."

"I was a plumber once, until I got hurt. Did you know that?"

"A plumber's helper, Chief – not a licensed plumber."

"It is the same. I could have put in the shower."

"I'm sure you could."

"And he wanted to leave after I paid him four hundred dollars."

"Really? What did you do?"

"I took the keys to his truck away from him and said he could not leave until he finished the job."

Jake looked at the size of the man in the apron cooking lobsters in the kitchen. "Chief, it pays to be six foot six and 370 pounds."

"Mmm."

Robert Paul laid out newspapers on the dining room table and put out two bottles of beer, hammers, forks, nutcrackers, and a dozen ears of Texas sweet corn with melted salt butter. After eight minutes, the lobsters turned a bright red and he pulled them out of the pot, setting them on the table. "Penny called," the big Wampanoag Indian said as they both sat down to dinner, "and some guy from 'Tech' was looking for you. Name was Dr. Harry Saver. I wrote his number by the kitchen phone. He said it was important and wants you to call him right away."

"I'll call Dr. Saver after dinner. What did Penny want?"

"Mmm," the Indian grunted again as was his practice when he did not want to answer Jake. "Who is this Dr. Saver guy from MIT, who called you at the house? He has a good name for a doctor."

"He's not that kind of doctor. Harry is our marine engineering expert for the ferry cases. He did a study on the *Katama's* steering, controls, power plant, engines, alarms and electronics for us."

"I bet you are paying him more than you pay me."

"Do you have a PhD in marine engineering?"

"No, but I know all about ferries. Remember, I worked on those boats for nearly twenty years until I got hurt."

"Yes, as a deckhand. I remember. What did Penny want?"

"She booked your car reservation to leave the island next Wednesday on the 5:00 a.m. ferry. You have a guaranteed return Wednesday night."

"The boys are flying in on the red eye next Wednesday. What time do they arrive?"

"They will be in Boston at 7:40 a.m. Wednesday morning. You have time to get them and go to the courthouse."

"Go to the courthouse? What courthouse?"

"That is the message from Penny. She said the clerk of the federal court in Boston put your ferry motion on the hearing list for Wednesday morning at ten o'clock."

"You mean my motion to quash the deposition subpoena?"

"Mmm."

"And that's the same morning the boys will arrive."

"Mmm."

*

Maggie Dellahunt thought it would be a good idea for their two boys to spend the summer with their father. He understood his drinking drove Maggie and the boys away. And there were the women. Unlike men, who are quick to forget and slow to forgive, Jake knew women forgave, but they never forget. He understood she could never completely trust him again, but did not want the boys growing up without knowing their father.

When Jake saw his two sons step off the ramp and walk past the gate, he could hardly hold back the tears. It had been more than five years since he had seen them, and they were everything he had imagined and more. They were four and nine when she cut him out of their lives. But now, at this very moment, all of his mistakes no longer mattered – only the two boys mattered.

As soon as they saw Jake and Robert Paul waiting for them, they rushed over to the big Indian first and hugged him openly with genuine affection. The Wampanoag was so tall they could only wrap their arms around each of his legs. He leaned over and held each of them to him with his huge hands. "It's been a long time. Your dad and me, we missed you like the rivers miss the rain."

Michael, Jake's nine-year-old, looked up. "We missed you, too, Uncle Big Chief."

The Wampanoag Indian's eyes grew misty. He released the boys and wiped a tear off his cheek with the back of his hand. "Me too, Michael and Little Jake."

Jake's fourteen-year-old stepped away and angrily yelled, "Don't call me, 'Little Jake.' I don't like that name."

The outburst took the Indian by surprise. "I am sorry you do not like being called, 'Little Jake.' What do you want us to call you now?"

"Anything, except, 'Little Jake.'"

"He changed his name to Jack," Michael quickly volunteered.

The two boys approached their father more circumspectly and, stopping in front of him, they held out their hands ready to shake his. They looked down at their sneakers and quietly said, "Hello, Father."

Jake dropped down on one knee and took each of their outstretched hands and drew them to him. He grabbed the boys and lifted them a few inches off the ground until they began squirming and begged him to let them go. Jake put them down with tears in his eyes. They looked at one another for a long moment. Michael smiled at his father, but his older son, Little Jake, who was now to be called, "Jack," just looked at his father as if he were a stranger.

As they walked down the concourse together to pick up their luggage, Jake thought it peculiar Little Jake, who'd known him longer than Michael, seemed more distant than his younger brother. Robert Paul broke the ice. "Your father has a special gift for the two of you."

Michael squealed with joy, "What did you get us? Tell us. Please."

"Don't act like a jerk, Mikey. Grow the hell up," Little Jake quickly taunted.

Michael's smile disappeared and tears filled his eyes. Jake stopped and looked at his older boy. Jake was careful to control the tone in his voice. "Jack, I don't know how you acted with your brother in Los Angeles, but when you're with me, I expect you to be kind to him. And one other thing you need to know. I don't tolerate bad manners or bad language."

"I didn't want to come here in the first place," Little Jake shouted insolently. "I want to get on a plane and go back to LA," he screamed loudly enough for passengers to stop and stare at him.

Jake heard the anger in the older boy's voice and carefully measured his response. "I'm not holding you here. You can leave anytime you want. Do you have money to buy a return ticket?"

"No."

"Then let's make a deal, Jack. I'll find you a job on the island. When you've got enough money to buy a return ticket, you can go back. But as long as you're living with us, I want you to promise to be nice to Michael."

"I'll think about it."

90

"You've got ten seconds."

"And then what? I'm not afraid of you."

"Not me, Jack. You don't have anything to fear from me. I'm going to ask Uncle Big Chief to show you how Wampanoag Indians punish disrespectful children. Are you ready, Chief?"

"Mmm."

Jack looked up at the big Indian. The gigantic Robert Paul began to move toward him with a fierce look on his face. "Little Jake-Jack is not the boy I remember."

Little Jake started back peddling. "Alright. It's a deal, Dad. Call him off. Please. I promise to be nice."

*

They marveled at the extravagantly lavish Federal Court building in Boston, an excessively opulent and gaudy high-rise overlooking Boston Harbor. Jake thought it was a far cry from their little brick courthouse in Edgartown. Except for public parking, each hallway, lobby, office, courtroom and chamber seemed five times bigger than necessary. There was no parking space close by the entrance, so Robert Paul dropped off Jake and the boys, and then waited for them. The boys followed Jake onto the elevator and, when the elevator doors opened onto the eleventh floor, they walked into Judge Infante's lobby. They stopped at a desk where security buzzed them in.

"Are these your sons, Jake?" United States Magistrate Ned Infante asked.

"This is Jack, age fourteen, and Michael is nine."

"Almost ten," Michael chirped in.

"This is Judge Infante, boys. We went to law school together."

"Are you going to be the judge in my dad's case?" Michael asked.

"No, it's going to be heard in the courtroom across the hall. You can go in and watch if you want. How does that sound, boys?"

Jack was quick to answer, "Boring."

Jake turned to his son. "I don't understand you, Jack. I thought you might like to see how the law works. See what I do. I thought it would be interesting."

"Not."

"Don't be rude, Jack. You don't have to go in. You can park yourself outside in the hallway if you want."

Jack stood up without a word and left the room.

"I'm sorry, Ned."

"I have two teenagers myself."

"I wish it were that uncomplicated."

Michael raised his hand as if he were in school asking permission to speak.

"Yes, Michael."

"I want to go into the courtroom and watch. Can I, Judge Infante?"

"Of course. I think you'll be more comfortable waiting for the call of the list in this room. I've got a hearing, so you can stay as long as you want."

*

When Jake stepped into courtroom 15A, he was surprised to see the same two NTSB investigators who had handed him a deposition subpoena on Lambert's Cove Beach. Federal Agents Thomas O'Rourke and Patrick Callahan sat alone in the back row of the gallery. Except for the two men from the NTSB, the back benches were empty. Jake wondered why the two agents were in the courtroom. Their findings were required by law to be kept confidential and their investigation secret. They had to submit their reports to the NTSB for approval, and only the agency was allowed to disclose the results of their investigation.

Jake shook his head in disgust. He had not prepared for an evidentiary hearing, and the two agents were the last thing he had expected to see. Behind the rail, where lawyers and parties sat, the chairs and tables had been carefully arranged. A court stenographer sat reading a transcript off to the side of the bench.

Steve Dichentis, general counsel to the Steamship Authority from the Wall Street law firm of Baker, Block and Benson (BB&B), sat at a table on one side of the bench along with Assistant General Counsel Steven Hutchinson, representing the National Transportation Safety Board. Jake Dellahunt and his son, Michael, took the two chairs at the other table.

Steve Dichentis looked at Michael. "Starting your associates kind of young, aren't you Dellahunt? Get 'em real cheap when they're only five years old."

"I'm almost ten and my dad is going to kick your ass, Mister."

Jake smiled. "Michael, where did you learn to talk like that?"

"Jack."

Steve Dichentis shot back, "The kid's got some big mouth, Jake."

"Too bad you don't have partners at BB&B as smart as this kid. Oh, but you do."

A clerk walked in holding a small file folder, followed by a pretty, blond-haired, diminutive woman, exquisitely dressed in black robes with a string of white pearls visibly accenting her black blouse. Jake immediately recognized US Magistrate, Marianne Pitcher. He had tangled with her when she was an assistant US Attorney in the civil division. She had never worked a day in her life on the other side of the street, but rather had made a career out of successfully banging heads for the feds defending civil law suits, which Washington rewarded by appointing her to US Magistrate. Jake still smarted from the hammering he took fifteen years ago when she beat the hell out of him in two cases, one where his client was run over by a postal truck and another after his client went blind ten days after taking a federally sponsored flu shot. This was not the magistrate he had hoped for, but it was the one he faced. All stood as she entered and remained standing until the bailiff declared the proceedings open.

US Magistrate Pitcher took a seat behind the bench and the clerk handed her the file. She glanced at Jake for a moment, then looked down at Michael and smiled. Jake thought Ed Infante might have tipped her off he was bringing his sons to watch him work. "There are two motions before this court, The National Transportation Safety Board's Motion to Compel Mr. Dellahunt's Oral Deposition and Mr. Dellahunt's Motion to Quash the NTSB's Deposition Subpoena."

First she turned to Steve Dichentis, general counsel for the Steamship Authority. "I am quite frankly surprised to see counsel for the Steamship Authority present. I would think the motions to compel and to quash the deposition subpoena are a matter solely between Mr. Dellahunt and the National Transportation Safety Board. It's the NTSB that wants this court to order Mr. Dellahunt's orally transcribed testimony."

Steve Dichentis started to stand, but the magistrate motioned him to remain seated. "This is just a motion hearing, so let's keep it informal for the moment."

"I believe we can clear the docket quickly," Dichentis began. "I have spoken with the counsel for the NTSB and they are in full agreement. If Mr. Dellahunt will agree to have this court appoint a federal arbitrator to make a full and final determination of negligence, the NTSB would be willing to tear up the deposition subpoena and drop any future objection to Mr. Dellahunt continuing as counsel of record. If the federal arbitrator fails to find the Steamship Authority negligent, the arbitrator's decision will be final and binding on all parties. That will put an end to all the negligence claims. If the arbitrator finds the Steamship Authority negligent, then the arbitrator will evaluate the amount each of Mr. Dellahunt's clients will recover."

Magistrate Pitcher nodded her head. "And the amounts of the awards, if any, will also be final and binding on all parties?"

"Yes, Your Honor. No appeals from the arbitrator's findings."

The magistrate shifted her attention to Jake. "What do you say, Mr. Dellahunt? Do you agree to arbitration rather than a trial?"

Jake heard the door open behind him and turned in time to see his older son enter the courtroom. The boy sat down in the same row beside the two federal agents. Jake returned his attention to the magistrate and hesitated long enough to make everyone wonder whether he understood what had just unfolded. He understood it well enough. If he agreed to trade a jury for a federal arbitrator, he could remain as counsel. If he didn't, Steve Dichentis would try to strip him of representation. Jake guessed Dichentis had somehow bagged, bought and owned the federal arbitrator. Why else was he so keen on keeping the case from being heard by a jury? He wondered if Magistrate Pitcher understood his dilemma.

There was an awkward silence and then the magistrate asked, "Would you like to speak to your clients? See what they would like to do? You don't have to give us your answer right away, Mr. Dellahunt. Take a week or ten days."

"I don't need ten days, Your Honor. I can tell you right now. I'll take my chances with a jury."

"You realize, of course, you won't be trying this case before any jury if I order your deposition and subject you to testifying in the case."

Jake stood up. "Experience tells me my clients will have a better chance of recovery in a courtroom than in a conference room. The last thing the Steamship Authority wants to do is put this case in front of a jury." Jake looked directly at Steve Dichentis. "They would love to have you order me to testify as a witness and thus disqualify me as counsel. There is one other thing, Your Honor, if I may."

The magistrate nodded.

"The two men sitting in the back row are the NTSB's principal investigators. They are the federal agents required to make findings of fact completely independent of any allegations or unsworn statements made in this courtroom today. If they are going to testify, I ask they be sequestered and leave this courtroom until called to testify."

"Are you calling either of these agents to testify at this motion session, Mr. Dichentis?"

"No, Your Honor."

"Perhaps you can explain to the Court why they are here."

Dichentis' face turned red. "I thought we might ..."

The magistrate was clearly chafed. "Stand up when you address the court, Mr. Dichentis. Do you understand my question?"

"I thought there might be a question about service of the deposition subpoena. They could attest to the fact service of the subpoena was in hand to Mr. Dellahunt."

Magistrate Pitcher nodded as if she understood what Dichentis was up to. "Did you see any pleadings about Mr. Dellahunt contesting service of the deposition subpoena, because I must have missed that part in my set of documents."

Dichentis was silent.

"You may sit down now, Mr. Dichentis, and the bailiff will remove the two agents from the courtroom."

As soon as the agents left, she turned to Jake. "I am acquainted with the general rule stating a lawyer shall not act as an advocate at a trial in which the lawyer is likely to be a necessary witness. If you are a necessary witness, Mr. Dellahunt, you will have to disqualify yourself or be disqualified by the court. Are you necessary to the defense of this case?"

"No, Your Honor, and there are several exceptions to that rule," Jake quickly responded.

"I am acquainted with the exceptions to the rule in cases where testimony would relate to an uncontested issue or the disqualification would work a substantial hardship on clients."

"Exactly right. I am arguing my testimony is unnecessary. I do not have any special, first-hand, personal knowledge in addition to any other witness. I am the only lawyer on the island who has practiced in courthouses around the United States for a large Boston law firm, and my experience and background make me indispensable to my clients."

"Are you saying there are no other qualified members of the bar to represent these plaintiffs on Martha's Vineyard?"

"I am saying it would work a substantial hardship on the plaintiffs because they would have to go off-island to find a trial lawyer with comparable experience. Last of all, I am asserting the deposition is nothing more than a fishing expedition to get at my work product, to find out what we have discovered to support theories of negligence, and to breach my duty of lawyer-client privilege." Of course, Jake knew he didn't have a shred of evidence to support his claims of negligence.

"You did witness the grounding of the ferry."

"As did Chief Robert Paul on our fishing boat, scores of other people on shore, as well as the passengers on the ferry. I'm unaware of anything more than they know."

Magistrate Pitcher looked back at the lawyers sitting at the other table. "Mr. Hutchinson, does the NTSB have anything to say?"

"Yes, Your Honor. We believe his proximity to the accident makes Mr. Dellahunt an indispensable witness. He was close enough to hear the crash alarms and loud speaker warnings, and to see the operational mechanics of the ferry and the condition of water, wind and tide. Those facts are in contest, and therefore we should be allowed to examine Mr. Dellahunt on such matters at deposition and trial. Also, there are at least five lawyers on the island who have practiced in the trial courts longer than Mr. Dellahunt and are capable of representing plaintiffs without posing any substantial hardship."

"Anything further?"

"I think that covers both exceptions to the rule."

The magistrate sat thoughtfully for a moment. Then she turned to the two lawyers sitting at the opposing table. Jake's heart skipped a beat because he knew judges look at the winners and rarely addressed the losers.

"The motions are unusual. On the one hand, the Steamship Authority has the right to examine all witnesses. But that right is not absolute. I find Mr. Dellahunt is not a necessary witness in these proceedings. I might point out, there was another witness on the boat with Mr. Dellahunt who is available to you. Anything he apparently witnessed related to the accident can be established through other witnesses, including the Wampanoag Tribal Chief, Robert Paul. Mr. Dellahunt brings us no special personal knowledge on issues related to negligence and I find forcing counsel to testify would disqualify him from representation and work a substantial hardship on his clients."

She then looked directly at Jake. "Therefore, I am going to allow you, Mr. Dellahunt, to continue representation in this matter. The NTSB's Motion to Compel the Deposition is denied. Mr. Dellahunt's Motion to Quash the Deposition Subpoena is allowed. However, I am going to separate issues of negligence from issues of damages. Therefore, I am bifurcating the cases into two separate trials, the first one on the issue of negligence and the next on the issue of damages. The first trial will determine if the Steamship Authority or their employees were negligent and caused the plaintiffs injury. If the jury makes a finding of negligence, there will be a second trial to determine the amount of money each of the injured parties will be paid. However, if the jury does not find the Authority negligent, there will be no need for a second trial."

"One other thing," she continued. "Trial will begin two weeks after the NTSB makes its findings." Magistrate Pitcher hammered her gavel on the bench, stood up and exited the courtroom, along with the clerk and the bailiff. Steve Dichentis and Steven Hutchinson said nothing, packed up and scurried out. Jake and Michael rose and left with Jack tagging along beside them. Michael stopped in the hallway. "Did we win, Dad?"

Jake thought a moment. "You were right, Michael. We kicked ass."

*

The weeks rolled by quickly. Jack worked pumping gas at the Black Dog boat dock and Jake practiced law at his office above the Grapes of Wrath bookstore. As much as Jake tried to reconnect with Jack, he could not chip away the thick coat of ice that blanketed their chilly relationship. When Jake tried to talk to his son, Jack turned his back on him. A wall of silence separated them and it was clear Jack only wanted to squirrel away enough money to buy a return ticket to Los Angeles.

Jake searched for hard evidence of negligence against the Steamship Authority, but came up empty. The marine engineer, Dr. Harry Saver, reported nothing was wrong with the boat's mechanics, power plant, steering mechanism, electronics, navigation, or the communications systems. All elements of the ferry were checked, rechecked, and functioned perfectly. The National Transportation Safety Board tested blood samples from Helmsman Bobby Nicholson and Captain Hugh McGreggor for drugs and alcohol, but found none. They both had more than twenty years of service on ferries and were close to retirement age. Their records were spotless. The Steamship Authority's attorney, Steve Dichentis had assured the NTSB the captain and the helmsman were in the wheelhouse at the time of the accident, and the engineer was at the controls in the engine room, but still they were unable to prevent the ferry from running aground.

Jake stopped at the Tisbury Post Office one morning and picked up the mail. He sat down in his office and shuffled through the envelopes without opening them. Only two envelopes interested him. He felt his blood pressure rise when he saw the first was from the National Transportation Safety Board. He opened it. The cover page was titled in bold lettering, "Preliminary Findings Regarding the Grounding of the *Motor Vessel Katama*." He skipped the preliminaries, turned to the summary on the last page and read the conclusions. "There was no human error, no negligence, and no mechanical failure that caused the *Katama* to run aground. Without other credible evidence, we attribute the accident to an Act of God that forced the *Katama* to ground."

Jake read no further. He put the report down. Not good news, Jake thought, and looked at the second envelope. It was a pencil-thin, legal-size manila envelope from the Federal Court in Boston. He opened the envelope carefully and pulled out a single sheet of paper. It was titled, "Court Order." As was his practice, he read the last paragraph first. "ORDER: Trial of the action of The Estate of Arthur Mayhew, et al. vs. Martha's Vineyard Steamship Authority will be held two weeks from this coming Friday on the sole issue of negligence, commencing at 10:00 a.m. Since all parties live in Martha's Vineyard, trial to be held in the Dukes County Superior Court in Edgartown, Massachusetts."

*

It was August and it hadn't stopped raining for three days. Each day the rain became heavier than the day before. The rain fell along the outside of the Edgartown courthouse as the last juror was selected and took her seat in the jury box. Bald, thin-lipped and wrinkled-faced, eighty year-old Judge Charles Zaneski, a no-nonsense judge with a reputation of having a love affair with big banks, big business and big insurance companies, had been hauled out of retirement, dusted off, and sent to the Vineyard to preside over the trial. It was obvious from the first moment Judge Zaneski took the bench, he didn't take kindly to being dispatched to an island courthouse where none of Jake's clients seemed to own a tie, dress shirt or suit jacket. The judge's difficulty remembering Jake's name ran a close second to his courthouse dress code.

"When we resume on Monday morning, I expect all of your clients to be dressed properly for court. Do you understand, Mr. uh, what's your name again?"

"Dellahunt."

"Don't bring a one of them back into my courtroom if they can't show the proper respect. Do you understand, counselor?"

When it came to remembering the names of the lawyers, Jake believed the judge had selective Alzheimer's. When he didn't confuse Jake's name with a group of Italian tenors at the Met, he simply called Jake, "Counselor" or "Uh, What's Your Name Again." As if that were not bad enough, Judge Zaneski called the Steamship Authority's lawyer, Steve Dichentis, by his first name. "Is that right, Steve?" or "Will you do this or that for the court, Steve?" or "Don't forget to have your exhibits marked, Steve," all of which Jake did not take as a promising sign. Before dismissing the impaneled jury for the weekend, he turned to Jake and warned, "Counsel is again advised to dress his clients in proper décor. Do you understand, Uh, What's Your Name Again?"

"Dellahunt. Jake Dellahunt."

"You don't have to repeat it. Adjourned until 9:00 a.m., Monday morning."

Jake took the pickup along the shore road to his office. As he drove along State Beach, the same questions nagged at him like a backseat driver. Why didn't the ferry captain warn the passengers? Why didn't he use the boat's loudspeakers? Why didn't he order the engineer to reverse engines? Sound the crash alarms? Why didn't the helmsman reduce speed or change direction? The answer was obvious to him. They were all doing something else, something they shouldn't have been doing.

It was a little before 4:00 when Jake parked his Ford pickup behind the Grapes of Wrath bookstore and climbed the stairs to his office. He dropped his trial bag and sat down in his wet raincoat.

Penny Pacheco took one look at the water he was tracking all over the floor and scolded him. "You're turning the waiting room into Lake Tashmoo with those wet shoes. Take off that raincoat and put those shoes next to the vent to dry out."

He peeled off his wet raincoat and placed his shoes on top of the warm air vents. He sat down in the swivel chair behind his desk and then went limp.

"So, what's the judge like?" she asked.

Jake preferred not to recount the day in the courthouse. Instead, he simply ran his worried fingers through his wet hair, trying to comb out the day's events. He bent over, opened his trial bag and pulled out a pile of papers. He pushed the papers toward her. "Take a gander at the gift Steve Dichentis handed me in court today."

Penny picked up the papers and scanned the title in bold letters: "*Final Report of the National Transportation Safety Board.*"

"Is this the first time you've seen the final report, boss?"

"The very first."

"Aren't you supposed to get it before the trial begins?"

"I pointed that out to the judge."

"What did he say?"

I think his exact words were, "Take the weekend to read it, Mr. Dellaguardia."

"Is that what he calls you?"

"That seems to be his favorite."

Penny looked back at the papers. "It says, 'a Proxigean Tide – an extraordinary confluence of current, tide and wind combined to drive the *Katama* outside the channel in West Chop and into the shoals west of Lambert's Cove.' What the heck is a Prox-i-something Tide?"

"A Proxigean Tide? It's that rarest of moments when the sun, moon and earth are all lined up to sink our case."

Penny saw no humor in Jake's answer. "Tell me, what does it really mean?"

"It means powerful waves of tide and current that leave ships helpless at sea."

She thought a moment. "Is that what you think happened to the ferry? The moon, earth and sun were all lined up?"

"Not me. I don't have the foggiest. It's them. They think the planets were all lined up at the precise moment of the ferry accident to create some kind of weird tsunami off West Chop, at a point exactly where the ferry was traveling. Some coincidence."

"I would say. Does this mean an end to our case?"

"If it's not the end, it's a celestial warning. You can't recover money damages for an astrophysical event. It's an act of God."

*

The following day was Saturday, and Jake and Penny started their morning early. Jake spent most of the time revising and memorizing the opening statement he planned to make to the jury. They were preparing witness examination topics and questions when the phone rang. Penny picked it up and handed the phone to Jake. It was Robert Paul. Jake heard the concern in the big Indian's voice. "Yes Robert, what's wrong?"

"I think you should come home, right away. Michael is running a high fever."

"Chief, there's a thermometer in the medicine cabinet. Did you take his temperature?"

"That is the reason I am calling. It's a hundred and four. He's burning up. Do you want me to call Franny Meezum, our tribal medicine man?"

"I'll be home in a few minutes."

"You know Franny can make the boy well. He knows more medicine than all the doctors on this island."

"I know he does, but I think his mother would prefer calling a traditional medical doctor. Look, I'll be home in five minutes. I'm leaving now."

"And one other thing."

"What is it, Chief?"

"This morning, Jack told me he had saved enough money over the last six weeks to leave."

"Let's deal with Michael first. I'm leaving right now."

Jake hung up and thought a moment. He fished his cell phone from his pocket and scrolled down to "received calls" until he recognized one number and hit the dial button. A familiar voice answered on the other end of the line. "Hello, this is Dr. Josephine Hayes speaking."

"Jo, this is Jake Dellahunt. I know this is kind of short notice, but what are you doing right now? I really could use a big favor."

*

It didn't take fifteen minutes for Dr. Josephine Hayes to meet Jake at the cottage. She took one look at Michael lying in bed in a pair of wooly pajamas soaked in sweat and stripped him naked, then wrapped him in cold, moist towels. She opened a bottle of Tylenol and gave him two pills with water. Then she sat on the edge of Michael's bed sponging his face and neck with cold compresses, while Jake brought in more cold towels to drape around the boy. After forty-five minutes, she stood up and took Michael's temperature once again.

She looked at the thermometer with satisfaction and nodded. She turned to Jake and said, "The fever's broken. His temperature is just under a hundred and one." She dried off Michael, put him under a clean sheet and let him close his eyes.

Waiting outside the bedroom, Robert Paul asked, "What is wrong with Michael, Doctor Hayes?"

"It's probably a flu. There's a summer virus going around. I'll leave you the children's Tylenol to reduce his fever and chills. I want him to drink a lot of fluids. He should be back to his old self in a few days. Make sure he drinks a lot."

Michael heard the doctor and opened his eyes. "Like Cokes, Dr. Hayes?"

She poked her head back into the room. "No sodas. Just fruit juice and water."

She turned to Jake. "If his temperature rises, call me. Any rashes, call me."

The big Indian said, "He's complaining of aches and pains. I am worried about Lyme disease."

"Yes, the ticks are out now. Do you check for ticks at least once a day?"

"I keep Michael out of tall grass and check him every morning and afternoon. I never see ticks on him. But they are so small."

"Not when they're engorged. I examined for swelling around the joints, redness and bites or signs. There's nothing. But keep a careful watch for any redness."

Robert Paul replied, "I will, Doctor." Then the big Wampanoag bent under the threshold, stepped into the hallway and motioned them to follow him onto the screened deck facing Lake Tashmoo. "I made a lobster salad. It is on the table. I will go back to Michael and watch him."

Jake smiled at the doctor. "Yes, please Jo. Please have lunch here. It's the very least we can do."

"Alright Jake, I would like that."

Robert Paul had set out two place settings of their best china and silverware on a white linen cloth. In the center of the deck table, a vase filled with bright, island blue Rosa Rugosas, wild Lady Slippers, and yellow petal Black Eyed Susans overflowed onto the tiny white petals of Queen Anne's lace. A bowl of chilled lobster salad sat beside two crystal wine glasses and a cold bottle of Island Chardonnay. Jake had orchestrated the lunch, but the chief had turned the medical house call into a romantic interlude.

Jo looked at the spread. "It's so beautiful, Jake. Tell me, are you trying to seduce me with lobster salad and wildflowers?"

Jake helped her into a chair. "Not a bad idea. I asked Robert to whip up something. He says I'm a lonely bachelor."

"Are you lonely? Did it take Michael's fever to get you to call me?"

"Not at all. I would have called you. It's just that I've been going nuts trying to find out what happened to the ferry."

"Some excuse for not calling a girl. It's always the guys you like who never call."

He opened the wine and filled her glass. "I haven't called anyone since we met. I swear I've been thinking about you, but I've been working on the ferry case."

"So, you've been thinking about me. Exactly what were you thinking, Mr. Dellahunt?"

He didn't answer. Instead, he poured himself half a glass and held up his glass to hers. "Thank you, Jo. Thank you for being here for us today."

She shook her head and smiled. "You're welcome. And thank you for lunch."

Her dimpled smile warmed his heart. "What do you think of Michael?"

"He's so sweet. You know, I met your other son, Jack."

"When?"

"At the boat dock, last week. One of the doctors invited a bunch of us from the hospital to go out on his boat. Jack was running the fuel pump and I had a chance to talk to him. He told me he was a movie star's son. I asked him who and he said Maggie Dellahunt. Then I told him I knew you."

"What did he say to that?"

"You don't want to know."

"He's still angry about the divorce. He's been saving up all summer to buy a return ticket to L.A. Robert told me today he's got enough to leave now."

"Do you want him to leave?"

"Of course not. But he hardly talks to me."

"Can I make a suggestion?"

"Sure."

"How old is Jack? Fourteen or fifteen? All boys do at his age is dream about girls."

"So do their fathers."

She laughed. "Not from where I'm sitting. Find him a girlfriend and watch him turn into a different person."

"Any suggestions?"

"My daughter, Melanie, is here on the island with me. She's fourteen and doesn't know a soul here. She usually spends the summers in the Berkshires with her dad."

"You were married?"

"To a lawyer for three years. Except for our daughter, it was a disaster. She is very special. I think Jack would like her."

"How about bringing her over for dinner tonight? You can look in on Michael and we can see how the other two kids get along."

She smiled once again. "Sounds like a plan for Jack and Melanie, but what are you doing after dinner? James Taylor is at the Outerland Club tonight."

"I'd love to go, but I really don't want to leave Michael."

"I understand. But Jacoby Dellahunt, you need to get out of the house and start enjoying life."

*

When Jack returned home, he walked past his father and straight to his room without a word. Jake followed him. "Jack, I want to speak to you. Dr. Hayes is bringing her daughter over for dinner. I want you to be nice to her."

Jack didn't respond. Jack's sullen look at his father said it all. "I'll skip dinner tonight, thank you. Anyhow, I have enough money to buy a plane ticket and go home."

"I know. Uncle Big Chief told me."

"You don't really care. It seems to me you spend most of your time figuring out how to win that ferry case of yours."

"I do care, Jack, a lot. But it's hard to have a conversation when you won't talk to me. You haven't said more than ten words to me in nearly two months."

"What's the point? You're always working on that stupid ferry accident case. You're never home much. It seems to me your lawyer stuff is more important than Mikey and me."

"Look Jack, I've tried to get through to you, but you won't let me. I don't know how many times I've asked you to go fishing with me."

"You know I work weekends, Dad. Remember?"

"We could have gone sailing together on your day off," Jake said quietly.

"And each time we made plans, you had to go to Boston or to the Edgartown courthouse or somewhere else for that case of yours."

"There are fifty-one people depending on me. It's a responsibility I take seriously. I hold their lives and fortunes in my hands. What could I do?"

"You could have paid more attention to your sons than your work," Jack replied and threw his hands up in desperation. "What's the use of talking?"

"What's the use? What's the use?" Jake repeated. "It's ... it's you're my son. I love you. I know I was a lousy father and lost you and Michael."

"More than lousy," Jack shouted and began to shake. "You were a boozer and screwed around until Mom couldn't take it anymore. You were the worst father in the world." Jack's eyes turned red and he looked away.

"I know. I am so sorry." Jake walked over to his son and tried to wipe the tears falling from the boy's cheeks. Jack pushed him away.

"Please Jack. People change. I've changed. Have you seen me do anything inappropriate since you've been here? Drinking or running around? Not one thing. All I'm asking is ... is for a second chance. Everyone's entitled to a second chance. Even me. Aren't I?"

*

Melanie Hayes was the most beautiful fourteen-year-old girl on the island that summer. She had the face of an angel and Jack couldn't take his eyes off of her throughout dinner. Jake thought Jo had been right. If Jack had any plans to leave the island, they were cancelled that night. After dinner, the big Indian piled the two kids in Jake's old pickup and drove them to the movies in Oak Bluffs while Jake and Jo stayed home to clean up and wash the dishes.

Jake was never big on appliances around the kitchen. He stood at the sink, dressed in the Indian's oversized apron, washing plates and silverware, and handing them to Jo to towel dry and stack in the cabinets above her. When she moved close, she brushed by him. He turned to her and kissed her ever so gently, their lips barely touching. She was intoxicating. He looked into her deliciously huge brown eyes.

She put her dish towel down and wrapped her arms around his neck. "Why Jake Dellahunt, I do believe this is the first time I have ever kissed anyone wearing an apron."

He took her in his arms. She was perfume and dish washing detergent, and he kissed her until she limply melted into him. His lips touched hers as he said, "I really wanted to call you. It's just that I've been working on the ferry case."

She held her lips to his. "I know. I heard about the Proxigean Tide thing. Do you believe it?"

He glued his lips to hers. "Mmm. I believe two celestial bodies can create some wicked strong magnetism."

"Heavenly bodies have some special attraction." She touched her lips to his and held them there. "Mmm. You know it would be unethical for me to talk about any patient."

He kissed her deeply. "I know."

Her lips touched the corners of his mouth. "I could lose my license if I divulged anything about a patient I treated. Mmm. For example, if I had treated a boat captain who became sick, let's say for example, maybe he suffered a heart attack, which I am not saying, but hypothetically … mmm, had a heart attack and stopped breathing … mmm, needed mouth to mouth from the only person around him while his boat crashed on shore, I couldn't tell you anything about it."

His lips were pressed to hers. "Yes, mouth to mouth. It would be unethical for a doctor to tell … mmm. If that happened, I mean hypothetically, wouldn't the information be in his medical chart?"

She kissed him. "Uh uh, no. No … not unless you knew what to look for. And then it's only a suggestion of a heart attack. Not real proof of when or where he had it. If he won't say he had a heart attack, no tests done … mmm, well there's nothing to show he did or didn't have an attack when the ferry had the accident."

He kissed her back. "Mmm … you're such a good doctor, Doctor."

"And you are such a good kisser, Mister."

Just then the kitchen door opened and Robert Paul walked in.

*

"Before I seat the jury for your opening statements, does either counsel have any pretrial matters that need to be heard? How about you, Steve?" Judge Zaneski asked off the bench Monday morning.

"Nothing for the defense, Your Honor," Dichentis replied.

Judge Zaneski looked at Jake. "And what about you, ah, counsel?"

Jake stood up. "I filed a motion this morning to compel production of Captain Stanley McGreggor's hospital records and gave a copy of my motion to Mr. Dichentis."

The clerk handed the motion papers to the judge, who quickly scanned the first page and then looked up.

"What's this about, Mr. Dellaguardia?"

"It's Mr. Dellahunt, Your Honor."

"Of course. Mr. Dellahunt. What's this about?"

"We discovered the captain may have had a heart attack during the time the ship ran aground. We need his medical records to corroborate it."

"Where did you get this information?" the judge asked.

Jake was not about to reveal his source. "We received the information over the weekend from someone in the hospital."

"But how reliable is this information?"

"That's why I need to see the medical records."

The judge looked at the table where Dichentis was sitting. "Do you have any objections, Steve?"

"I do, Judge. Mr. Dellahunt had plenty of time to file this motion, but waited for the last moment to ask for the captain's medical records. The time for discovery ended weeks ago. In either case, the medical records of a non-party are privileged. The captain has not been named as a defendant in this case."

Judge Zaneski nodded. "That's true."

Jake wasn't about to give up. "But the captain is an employee of the defendant Steamship Authority. As such, he is a party for purposes of obtaining records."

The judge quickly responded, "So you're saying if I sue General Motors, I can get any medical record of any employee on the assembly line I want? Is that your argument?"

"You certainly see the difference between the operator of a ship that has run aground and someone on the assembly line, unrelated to issues of a trial. And if the person on the assembly line was responsible for a part that failed and caused injury, yes, I believe his medical records can be examined."

"That may be true, but the time for filing motions, like this one for discovery, ended weeks ago. I am denying your motion on the basis it is beyond the permissible filing period."

Jake looked at the judge. "Then we will subpoena Captain Stanley McGreggor to testify for the plaintiffs' case in chief and order him to bring his records with him by *subpoena ducem tecet.*"

The judge did not hesitate to respond. "That's your right, young man, but the defense can move to quash that kind of subpoena for the same reasons. What you can't get through the front door, I am not going to allow you to sneak through the back door."

Jake sat down without showing any emotion. If Jake had learned anything about a courtroom, it was to never show pain or disappointment.

*

Once the jury took their seats, the judge nodded to Jake. "You may begin your opening statement."

Jake rose and stood before the jury. "Ladies and gentlemen of the jury, many of you traveled some distance to the island so we could select a fair and unbiased jury. On behalf of the fifty-one plaintiffs in this case, I want to thank you for taking time off from

111

your work and sacrificing precious time away from your families to serve our island community. This is a civil lawsuit, a case of negligence, and the only issue before us is whether the Steamship Authority failed to exercise reasonable care and diligence. We're not here to assess monetary damages. You're here only to decide whether the Steamship Authority, or any of its employees, is guilty of negligence. For my part, I am going to be as brief as possible."

Jake left the plaintiff's table and walked over to the jury box where he stood with his hands on the rail, making eye contact with each juror. "This case is about two words, 'Proxigean Tide.' I expect the Steamship Authority's lawyer, sitting over there, is going to try to sell you a bill of goods that it was the Proxigean Tide that caused the *Katama* to run aground. He will weave a delightful tale about a moment when the sun, moon and earth were all lined up at precisely the same time to create some sort of magnetic force aimed directly at a tiny point in the Atlantic Ocean where the *Katama* just happened to be located. He will wave his magic wand to resurrect the enchanted forces which pushed the *Katama* off course, causing the ferry suddenly to run aground and thereby severely injuring many and killing one passenger. The Steamship Authority's lawyer will try to persuade you this was an astronomical event, an act of God, a freak accident of nature for which they have no responsibility, no liability, and no culpability. He will insist they cannot be held negligent for something caused by natural forces. He will parade the findings of the Transportation Safety Board in front of you. He will give you evidence all the mechanical and electronic gear on the *Katama* were a hundred and fifty percent operational and in perfect running condition. He will provide you with evidence that the captain and his crew were working at maximum efficiency."

Jake walked back to the center of the well. "Well, if all that were true, why didn't the captain warn the passengers the boat was being swept onto shore? Why didn't he use the boat's loudspeakers? Sound the crash alarm? Why didn't he order the engineer to reverse engines? Why didn't the helmsman reduce speed or change direction? Why didn't they do something, anything, to avert this tragedy? Why didn't they act when they had the last best chance to avoid the accident?

"The answer is obvious. They were doing something else. Something they shouldn't have been doing." Jake took a step away from the jury. "If you buy into the fiction a Proxigean Tide caused the crash, ask yourself why weren't they aware of the impending astronomical event before they left the dock on the mainland? There was a ton of information about the Proxigean Tide available in the marine advisories that day. Again, the conclusion is inescapable. They didn't bother reading current and tide predictors, tide logs, charts and other marine warnings for exceptional tides and currents in and along Vineyard Sound. Natural forces weren't responsible for this catastrophic grounding. A series of human errors caused these tragic injuries. By the end of the case, you will have marshaled more than enough facts to find the Martha's Vineyard Steamship Authority failed to act reasonably. At the end of this case, I am confident you will find them negligent."

Jake thanked the jury for their attention, walked past Steve Dichentis with a little nod and sat down. The judge looked at Steve Dichentis. "Does the defendant, Martha's Vineyard Steamship Authority, wish to make an opening statement or would you prefer to reserve until the time of your defense?"

Dichentis stood up and dug both his hands in his pant pockets. "If it please, Your Honor, I am not going to let a minute go by without putting this matter straight in the jury's minds. I don't want Mr. Dellahunt to hoodwink this jury for one second. I would like to make my opening now. I promise it will be brief and to the point."

Dichentis took his hands out of his pockets and stood silently in the well for a moment. "Ladies and gentlemen of the jury, there is an independent federal agency made up of men and women who spend years studying accidents. They are members of the National

Transportation Safety Board. They go to schools and travel to places all over the face of the earth to study the nature and causes of accidents. They eat, sleep and spend most of their working days investigating ship, plane, and train accidents. These dedicated men and women examine accident scenes and reconstruct wrecks with microscopic precision. They are our front line investigators, who travel around the world, search debris for clues, interview witnesses, and re-enact events leading to an accident. They consider every possible cause, every factor that contributes to each tragedy, no matter how insignificant.

"Their investigations are completely independent of the Justice Department or any other federal or state agency. They are free of any outside bias and are sworn to conduct investigations in complete secrecy. They are forbidden by federal law to have contact with anyone outside their agency. That means no outside experts, no contact with lawyers, nobody except those within their own agency. At the end of their secret investigation, what was the government's final conclusion? The investigators found a Proxigean Tide caused the *Katama* to run aground onto the shoals off Martha's Vineyard.

"You will learn from the investigators in this case, Federal Agent Thomas O'Rourke and his partner, Patrick Callahan, when the sun, moon and Earth are lined up, it can create an unusual condition in nature, often referred to as a Proxigean Tide. They will testify this Proxigean Tide, this aberrant force of nature, can and did cause a cataclysmic event that carried the ferry out of the channel and forced it to ground.

"What you have just heard from Mr. Dellahunt is neither factual nor true. A Proxigean Tide is a split-second event. Nobody knows exactly where or when it will strike. It lasts momentarily and then disappears. Before we finish, you will be convinced the event was instantaneous, Captain McGreggor did not have time to sound alarms, warn the passengers, nor maneuver the *Katama* away from shore. And while the charts did predict a Proxigean

Tide, nobody, including the people who wrote the warnings, knew exactly where or when it was going to strike that day. After hearing all of the evidence, I am sure you will find the accident was caused by natural forces and the defendant, Martha's Vineyard Steamship Authority, is completely free of negligence."

*

"Call your first witness, Mr. Dellaguardia."

Jake's eyes ran up to the first name on his witness list. "Plaintiffs call Barney Till."

A short, elderly man in an ill-fitting suit climbed into the witness box. The clerk swore him in and asked, "State you name and address for the court."

"My name is Barney Till and I live at 38 McClellan Street in Plymouth, Massachusetts."

Jake stood up and leaned against the edge of the plaintiff's table. "Mr. Till, are you a plaintiff in this case?"

"What do you mean?"

"Are you a party in this lawsuit, sir?"

"Naw, I was just on the ferry *Katama* when she happened to run aground."

"Did you receive a summons to testify in this case?"

"I wouldn't be here if I didn't."

"Just answer the questions," Judge Zaneski ordered.

"Sorry, Your Honor. Yes, I'm here because your law office summoned me."

"You said you were on the *Katama* when it ran aground. Exactly where were you on the ferry when it crashed?"

"I was outside on the upper deck, watching the ferry move out of the channel."

"How do you know it left the channel?"

"I take the ferry to visit my sister once a week and I know where the channel markers are placed. The red channel markers lead the way into the harbor. One moment, the ferry was on the right of the marker and then next moment it was on the wrong side moving toward the shoals. Then all hell broke loose."

"About how much time passed from the time it left the channel to the time, in your words, when 'all hell broke loose?'"

"Maybe a couple of seconds."

"Could you give us the time in seconds if I counted the seconds for you?"

"Yes, I believe I could."

"Stop me as I count out seconds from my watch, beginning now. One-one thousand, two-one thousand, three-one thousand, four-one thousand, five ..."

"Stop."

"Less than five seconds."

"Yes."

"And in those five seconds, did you hear any alarms or loudspeakers or other warning?"

"No."

"Did the boat slow up or change direction?"

"No."

"Did you see the captain or the helmsman after the boat ran aground?"

"No. All I saw were a lot of injured people and I spent my time trying to help them."

"Thank you, Mr. Till. That's all I have at this time."

The judge looked at the defense table. "Mr. Dichentis, you may cross-examine."

Steve Dichentis stood up and leaned over the defense table toward the witness, with his hands on the table. "Mr. Till, do you know what caused the *Katama* to run aground?"

"I thought that was what this trial was about."

The gallery laughed and Jake smiled at the answer.

"Please answer my question. Do you know what caused the accident?"

"No, sir."

"But you think it might have been as much as five seconds from the time the boat left the channel to the time it ran aground."

"Five seconds, yes sir."

"Could it have been less than five?"

"Maybe, but I would say five is about right."

"Thank you. I have nothing further."

The judge looked up. "You are excused, Mr. Till. Call your next witness, Mr. Dellahunt."

"Plaintiffs call Perry Chapman."

The clerk looked around and then called out Perry Chapman's name twice.

A tall man wearing an open-collar shirt and blue blazer walked into the courtroom. The clerk swore him.

Jake rose to his feet. "Mr. Chapman, did you have occasion to be on the ferry boat *Katama* when it went aground?"

Before the witness could answer, Steve Dichentis was on his feet. "I believe this is a repetitive witness, Your Honor."

"Do you have an objection?" the judge asked.

"I do, Your Honor."

"Sidebar," the judge ordered, and both lawyers moved to the side of the judge's bench where they could not be overheard by the jury. "What is your objection, Steve?"

"Including this witness, Mr. Dellahunt has listed twenty-one other witnesses who were on the *Katama* at the time of the accident. If he seeks the same information we just heard from Mr. Till, we could save the court a considerable amount of time."

The judge turned to Jake. "Are you seeking the same information from these witnesses?"

"I want to establish there were no alarms, loudspeakers, or any warning of the impending disaster; no change of speed or direction and it took at least five seconds from the time the boat left the channel to the time it ran aground."

Dichentis then said, "No need to call all those witnesses. We'll stipulate to those facts."

The judge thought a moment. "Alright, step away from the bench and take your seats."

"Ladies and gentlemen of the jury, counsel for the Martha's Vineyard Steamship Authority and for the fifty-one plaintiffs bringing this lawsuit have agreed to stipulate there were no alarms, loudspeakers, or any warning of the impending disaster; no change of speed or direction of the *Katama* before the accident, and it took at least five seconds from the time the boat left the channel to the time it ran aground. Those facts are not in contest and both parties have agreed you take into consideration those facts as undisputed."

The judge looked at the witness. "You may step down, Mr. Chapman. This may be a good time to take our lunch break. We'll resume at 2:00 p.m."

Jake looked at his watch. Uncle Big Chief would be home watching Michael and there was plenty of time to have lunch with them at the cottage. He called Penny and asked her to join them for lunch.

*

Jake lifted Michael and sat him next to Penny at the picnic table on the back deck. "How are you doing, Tiger. Feeling better?"

"Uncle Big Chief says I'm back to normal."

Robert Paul brought out a pitcher of cold lemonade, freshly baked bread and a platter of cold fish salad. He then took his seat at the table opposite Michael. "He has been beating me at Scrabble all morning."

"Dad, is there a word, *'wampeyaunum'* in English? Uncle Big Chief says there is. I think he cheats."

"It means white dog," Robert Paul explained.

Jake laughed. "English words only, Chief. No Wampanoag."

As they began their lunch, there was a momentary lull in the conversation. Just then, Jack stepped onto the deck and smiled. It was the first time Jake had seen the sunshine on his son's face and it warmed his heart. Jake drank in his son's bright, new, smiling face. Melanie Hayes left Jack with the same perpetual smile Jake remembered seeing when he once looked in a mirror, after he fell in love with fourteen-year-old Peggy Dorgan.

"I have a few hours off and thought I would come home for lunch. Got enough food, Uncle Big Chief?" Jack asked.

Robert Paul stood up. "I made enough to feed all of us and half the seagulls on the island. The gulls will have a little less for lunch. Take a seat, Jack."

Jack turned to his father. "I thought you were in court, Dad."

"The judge sent us home for lunch, so I thought I would check on Michael. I have to go back in about an hour."

"How is the case going?" Jack asked.

"Hard to say."

"Dad is going to kick their ass – you'll see, Jack."

"Michael."

"Sorry, Dad, but it's true," Michael grinned.

"Who is your next witness?" Penny asked.

"Captain Hugh McGreggor, the ferry captain."

"Are you going to ask him about the heart attack?" she inquired quickly.

"There's an unwritten rule you don't ask a witness a question if you don't know the answer."

"But you have his hospital records, don't you, boss?" Penny suggested.

"The judge is sitting on them. He won't let McGreggor's hospital records in. Asking the captain if he had a heart attack could be dangerous. If he denies he has a bum ticker, we don't have his records to impeach him."

Jack was following the conversation carefully. "Can I ask a dumb question? What happens if he admits he had a heart attack?"

Jake smiled at his son. "Well then, won't Steve Dichentis and the two investigators from the NTSB be surprised it wasn't the Proxigean Tide that caused the accident."

"If he admits he had a heart attack, do you think it's going to help our case?" Penny asked.

"Better than the sun, moon and stars."

Jack thought a moment. "Dad, I'm missing something. Where's the negligence if the captain had a heart attack? How can the captain be responsible for the crash because he had a heart attack?"

"You're right, son. You'd make a hell of a lawyer. There's no case if he had a heart attack. It's called a 'sudden emergency defense.' You can't be responsible for an accident if you suddenly fall ill."

"So the case is over."

"Not so fast. What if he didn't take his heart pills or tell the steamship authority he was at risk? Didn't go for treatment?"

"First you have to show he had a heart attack and then you have to prove he knew he was sick and wasn't taking his medicine. It sounds like a lot to prove." Jack thought a moment. "I don't think it's a very good case."

"I'm glad I didn't put you on the jury, Jack."

*

Captain Hugh McGreggor was surprisingly tall, ruddy faced and dressed in khakis with braids on both shoulders. A shock of gray hair fell over his forehead, accenting his blue eyes that did not betray a hint of anxiety. He took the stand unsmiling, hiding any trace of emotion. His voice was almost mechanical. "My name is Captain Hugh McGreggor and I live on 15 Front Street in Vineyard Haven."

Jake stood up and began his examination. "How many years of service do you have with the Martha's Vineyard Steamship Authority?"

"Twenty years."

"Do you plan to stay or retire?"

"I have put in my retirement papers."

"Were you the officer in charge of the *Katama* on the day it ran aground?"

"I was the ship's captain on the date of the accident."

"So you were the person in charge of the ferry."

"I was the person responsible for the safety of the passengers, crew and boat."

Jake looked up at the judge. He needed to ask leading questions. "Permission to treat the witness as hostile, Your Honor."

"Granted," Judge Zaneski replied.

"Were you in the wheelhouse when the ship left the channel off of Lambert's Cove?"

"I was."

"Exactly when did you become aware the boat had left the channel?"

"It all happened so fast. One moment the boat was in the channel and a moment later it was on the shoals. I could both see and feel the boat move sideways almost immediately."

"Did you try to change direction back into the channel?"

"We turned the wheel, but the boat did not respond."

"Do you know the boat's rudder was examined after the crash and it was perfectly amidships? It showed sign of being turned."

"Yes."

"Did you order the engines stopped or reversed?"

"There wasn't time."

"Did you change the speed or direction of the *Katama* before the accident?"

"No."

"Did you sound the crash alarm or give any warning of the coming crash?"

"As I said, there wasn't enough time."

"Wasn't the ship's horn just above the wheel? The crash alarm right in front of you on the ship's console?"

"Yes."

"It wouldn't have taken a second to hit the alarm button or sound the ship's horn?"

Dichentis was again back on his feet. "Objection! Calls for speculation."

Jake turned to the judge. "The witness has twenty years of experience in the wheelhouse. He's well aware of the amount of time it takes to sound the ship's horn or hit the crash button."

Judge Zaneski thought a moment. "You may have it. Overruled. Repeat your question, counsel."

"Would it take more than a second or two to sound the ship's horn or hit the crash warning button?"

"Probably not."

Jake returned to the plaintiff's table. "Are you here as a result of being served a *subpoena ducem tecet* my office sent you?"

"Yes, I received your subpoena."

"Ordering you to bring with you certain documents, correct?"

"Yes."

Jake pulled the list from a pile of papers on the table. He eyed the list. "Did you bring a copy of the ship's log with you?"

"Yes."

"The ship engineer's report?"

"Yes."

"A copy of Chapman's notes, and tide and current for that day?"

"Yes."

"A copy of your written account of the accident to the NTSB?"

"Yes."

"A copy of your written account of the accident to the Coast Guard?"

"Yes."

"Did you bring a copy of your hospital records?"

"On advice of counsel, I was told not to bring my hospital records to court."

Jake put his list down and walked to the furthest end of the jury box. "You mean, Steve Dichentis told you not to show up with your hospital records?"

Steve Dichentis was on his feet. "Objection! We went over this matter earlier, Your Honor."

Judge Zaneski waived at Dichentis to sit down. "He hasn't called for the records. Are you going to call for the captain's hospital records, Mr. Dellaguardia?"

"Yes, Your Honor."

"Then the objection is sustained. Jury will disregard the question and answer. Move on uh, counsel."

Jake turned and walked to the jury rail, and asked, "So let me understand this. You brought in the ship's log, the engineer's report, the tide and current advisories, your written account of the accident to both the Coast Guard and the National Transportation Safety Board, but you did not bring in your hospital records. Is there some reason you brought in everything but your hospital records?"

Dichentis jumped up. "Objection! Don't answer that question."

"Sustained. Let's move on," the judge ruled.

"Did you go to the Vineyard Hospital after the accident?"

"Yes."

"Were you seen by any doctors there?"

"Yes."

"For chest pain?"

Dichentis was on his feet again. "Objection. Only a doctor would know what was wrong with him. He's a ship captain, not a medical expert."

Jake did not wait for the judge to rule. "He should know how he felt when he went to the hospital."

Judge Zaneski nodded. "I agree. You may have the question."

"Did you have chest pain or any pain radiating down your arms when you went to the hospital?"

"Objection."

"Overruled."

Captain McGreggor took his eyes off Jake and looked at Steve Dichentis for help. It was a desperate look that sent Jake a message.

"Do you understand my question?" Jake asked, knowing Captain McGreggor understood the question only too well. "Did you have chest pain or any pain radiating down your arms when you went to the hospital?"

"No, I did not have any chest pain when I went to the hospital."

"You went to the hospital for some other reason?"

"Everyone pretty much went as a precaution."

"I see. You testified earlier you were about to retire. How's your health, Captain McGreggor?"

Dichentis was still standing. "Objection. Relevance."

The judge looked at Jake. "Counsel, can you connect up this line of questioning to the cause of the crash?"

"If I had his medical records before me, I might."

Judge Zaneski's face turned red. "One more question about this witness' health or hospital records, and I will hold you in contempt."

Jake knew he had antagonized Zaneski, but he was certain the jury got the message.

*

"I heard you were awesome in court today," Jack said as the boys helped Jake with the dinner dishes that evening.

"Thanks," Jake laughed. He could not believe how fast word traveled on the island.

Jack picked up a dish towel and began wiping. "Dad, did Captain McGreggor ever cop to having a heart attack?"

Jake smiled at his son's newfound interest. "No, but I'm sure something happened in that wheelhouse. It wasn't what he said as much as how he looked when he denied it."

Jack handed Michael a plate. "What do you mean?"

"He looked to Steve Dichentis for help before answering."

"Yeah, I remember Mr. Dichentis! We saw him in Boston the day we flew into Logan."

Jake handed another plate to Jack and started on the pans. "He's the Steamship Authority's lawyer."

"He thought I was five years old. What a jerk!" Michael squealed.

"Yeah, kind of a sleaze ball as I remember him now," Jack agreed. "He has a big power boat. I gas it up at the dock when he comes in with those other two guys."

Jake stopped washing. "What other two guys?"

"The two other guys who were in court with us in Boston. They sat right next to me until the judge tossed them out."

Jake turned off the water. "You mean O'Rourke and Callahan from the National Transportation Safety Board?"

Jack was still thinking about seeing them on the boat dock. "And some really butt ugly babes. They were so high they were floating."

"Let me get this straight. You're saying the two federal agents were partying with Dichentis and some women?"

"Yes, is it important?"

"Hell, yes."

"If it will help, I'm willing to testify I saw them all together on the lawyer's boat and more than once."

"How come you never mentioned it to me?"

"I never thought it was important, and besides we weren't talking. Remember?"

"I'm sorry, son, but I don't think anyone on the jury is going to pay too much attention to what the lawyer's son has to say."

Jack put down his dish towel. "Hey, I can prove it. The dude who runs the dock operation doesn't trust anyone. He's got cameras that catch everything that happens 24/7 on the dock, but he'll never give you the recordings. He's buddy-buddy with the lawyer for the steamship authority. What are you going to do?"

"Finish doing the dishes."

"That's it?"

"After we get the dishes put away, let's call Penny. I want you to talk to her."

*

The judge asked the two lawyers up to the bench before calling in the jury. "Who are those four young people sitting in the first row of my courtroom dressed in Bermuda shorts and t-shirts, Mr. Dellaguardia? I warned you about dress codes," the judge began.

Steve Dichentis turned around to look at them.

Jake smiled at the judge. "Not just t-shirts and Bermuda shorts, Your Honor. They are Boat Dock T-shirts. They are in uniforms they wear working at the dock when they fuel boats. You allowed Captain McGreggor to testify in his uniform. I didn't think you would find any problem with having the dock boys in the courtroom in their work clothes."

"Do you intend to call them?"

"I may if necessary, but only for rebuttal testimony against the next witness I intend to call."

Dichentis was still staring at the four dock boys. His face had gone chalk white. "I object. They are not on the plaintiffs' witness list."

"They don't have to be. I intend to call them as rebuttal witnesses against NTSB Agents O'Rourke and Callahan."

Judge Zaneski looked at Dichentis. "He is within his right to call rebuttal witnesses without notifying you. Now step back and call your next witness."

Dichentis faced the judge. "I move for a brief continuance, Your Honor."

Jake turned to Dichentis. "Aren't you feeling well, Steve? You look very pale to me."

"I am not feeling well, Your Honor. Just give me a half hour or so."

Jake finished the sentence. "To talk to those young men. One of them is my son. Do you really want them to forget seeing you partying on your boat with the federal investigators in this case and banging a bunch of hookers?"

The judge shook his head and wagged his finger at Dichentis. "I will excuse you for the day. Witness tampering is a federal offense. Neither you nor the investigators will have any contact with Mr. Dellahunt's four rebuttal witnesses. Do you understand, Mr. Dichentis? Step back."

For the first time, Jake heard the contempt in the judge's voice and it was directed at Steve Dichentis. "We will resume at 10:00 a.m. tomorrow. All scheduled witnesses, rebuttal witnesses and parties are ordered to be here on time and properly attired. Adjourned."

*

"You're in a good mood this evening, Papa."

"Thanks to my new junior partner."

"Pretty slick how you faked out Dichentis today."

"Penny actually produced the other dock boys out of thin air. Don't ask me how she did it, but it didn't take Dichentis an hour to throw in the towel."

"What is going to happen to him?"

"Nothing. O'Rourke and Callahan are going to take plenty of heat from the National Transportation Safety Board for being chumps when they get back to Washington."

"And what happens to the case?"

"The first part of the case is over. Dichentis would never want the stink of suborning Proxigean perjury to come out. He filed an agreement for judgment this afternoon. It's a finding the Martha's Vineyard Steamship Authority neither admits nor denies liability, but agrees to have a jury determine the amounts of money each passenger will be paid."

"Does that legal garbage mean they were guilty of negligence?"

"Exactly, but it's good garbage for us."

"So now what?"

"Another jury trial this winter determines how much to pay our people, leaving one last question."

"What's that?"

"What really happened in the wheelhouse that day?"

"Who cares? You won, didn't you?"

"I care."

"I have a question for you."

"Shoot, son."

"I switched workdays with a friend and Dr. Hayes is bringing over Melanie tomorrow. I wanted to take her out on the jet ski, just the two of us. Not with Uncle Big Chief watching all the time. Three's kind of a crowd, if you know what I mean. So, can we go out alone?"

Jake thought back thirty years to the moment when he took fourteen-year-old Peggy Dorgan behind the rocks in Oak Bluffs and first kissed her. "Sure, you deserve some time alone. You've been working hard. Just stay inside the inlet and tool around the lake."

"Thanks Dad. Really, thanks."

"Just promise me you'll be careful."

"I will," Jack said and ran into his room to call Melanie.

"And both of you wear your life gear," Jake shouted, but Jack had already closed the door to his room.

When Jake finished the dishes, he dialed Robert Paul on his cell phone. "Robert, I just gave Jack permission to take Melanie Hayes on the jet ski inside the jetty tomorrow. Give him the keys and please keep an eye on them. They want to be alone, so play at being the silent, unseen Indian I know you are. One more thing: I don't want them leaving the lake and going out into ocean."

"Okay, Jake. When will you be home tomorrow?"

"No later than four, and call me if there's a problem. Text me if I have to go back to court."

"I don't know how to do this text thing."

"Ask Michael to show you on his cell phone. He knows."

*

The next morning, Jake signed the paperwork in Edgartown without a hitch and Judge Zaneski dismissed the jury with thanks. Dichentis threw Jake serial daggers throughout the proceedings and then raced out of the courtroom to catch the next plane back to New York.

Jake took the shore road back to his office above the Grapes of Wrath Bookstore. He walked into the waiting room only to find Penny typing like mad on the computer. "Tell me, Ms. Penny Pacheco, did any of those three other boys, who showed up in court yesterday, ever work for one second at the Black Dog Boat Dock?"

"Not a stitch of time. Just your son, Jack."

"Where did you find those kids, central casting? Because they sure looked authentic."

"They are the three stock boys at Cronig's Market. Getting the boys wasn't a problem. It took most of Sunday to find three sets of Boat Dock T-shirts and Bermuda shorts that matched Jack's outfit and fit them."

"They certainly looked like dock boys."

"They were supposed to," Penny agreed. "What would you have done if Dichentis called your bluff and let the two NTSB investigators take the stand?"

"I have it on good authority there are videos of Dichentis, O'Rourke and Callahan whooping it up with a bunch of hookers. I suppose we'd have to bring in the FBI to get the recordings. Anyway, those two weren't going to lie on the stand. They would have taken the fifth. In the end, it was booze and hookers that sunk their ship."

Penny smiled. "You mean sunk their ferry boat. So, it was a case of negligence after all?"

Jake thought about it a moment. "Well, if it wasn't the Proxigean Tide, what the hell was it? I'm voting for a heart attack in the wheelhouse."

"Do you know Hugh McGreggor?"

"No, not really."

"He was the captain of the Vineyard High School football team, class president, went to the Coast Guard Academy in New London and was a highly-decorated naval officer. Everyone on this island knows him. He's a hero. We love the man. If he had a heart condition, he would admit it on the witness stand. He would never put his passengers at risk."

"He was months away from retirement when the accident happened. Maybe he gambled on getting a gold watch and full pension."

"If our clients thought he had a heart attack, they wouldn't have sued. They'd send him get-well cards and flowers."

"Not if they found out he wasn't taking his heart pills or didn't see a cardiologist. And it's not a case against McGreggor; it's a case against the Martha's Vineyard Steamship Authority."

Before Penny could respond, the phone rang. The number on the display was the landline at his house. It was Robert Paul and he was upset. "Jack took his girlfriend through the inlet and straight into the ocean. It's rough out there today. I am here alone with Michael. What do you want me to do?"

"Were they in floatation devices?"

"Life vests are attached to the jet ski ignition system. They have to wear them to run the boat."

"Then stay calm and watch Michael. Warm up the Mako. I'll be home in five minutes to deal with Jack."

*

Jake spent the next three hours on the Mako 22, combing through the ocean and beaches outside of the inlet. As soon as he left the shelter of Lake Tashmoo, the wind and waves picked up and bounced the Mako through the air, crashing the hull into the sea.

Jake slowed the boat to give it better stability in the heavy seas and he thought about the kids being tossed around in a ten-foot open jet ski. He followed the north side of West Chop into the harbor and then reversed direction off of East Chop going into Vineyard Sound until he almost lost sight of the island. He reversed direction and traveled along the northwest side of the island opposite the Elizabeth Islands until his fuel gauge began to move toward empty. After another half hour of searching, he turned back toward the Lake Tashmoo inlet and pulled out his cell phone.

"Chief, I've come up empty. Have you heard anything?"

"Nothing. We should call the Coast Guard."

"Call them now, and please call Dr. Hayes at the hospital. Tell her what's happened."

"Do you want me to call Maggie in Los Angeles?"

"No, I'll call her as soon as I get home."

*

Jake quickly tied the Mako to the dock and hurried along the sandy path to the Mathews' Cottage. As he made his way through the path surrounded by beach plums and sea grass, he could see a white pickup between the salt water pines making its way up Cottage Road. He thought it must be Jo Hayes. He dreaded telling her he had not found any trace of the kids or the boat. The pickup slowed and turned into the driveway. As it drew closer, he recognized blue and red Coast Guard stripes on the doors when it stopped in front of the cottage. His heart skipped a beat as he saw Jack and Melanie step out of the back doors followed by the driver, a young man dressed in his Coast Guard khakis. The jet ski was tucked into the truck bed and tied down.

Seeing Jack and Melanie brought a rush of tears to Jake's eyes. He was surprised by his own emotions. Relief replaced worry and anger. He ran to Jack and hugged him. He swung him around in circles like a five-year-old. Then he dropped him and hugged Melanie gently. Still overcome with joy, he said, "If I weren't so happy to see the two of you, I would really be pissed. The whole island has been out looking for both of you. I've been half out of my mind with worry." Jake wiped the tears from his eyes. "Where have you been?"

Neither Jack nor Melanie said a word, but the look on their faces said it all. Jake knew what they were probably up to. He looked at his son and smiled. "Jack, I'm glad you're home."

Jack's eyes began to tear. His voice had choked up. "I'm so sorry. I know I promised to stay in the lake, but I don't know. We just lost track of time. That's all. And Dad, I'm sorry for everything I did this summer. There's never been a day gone by I haven't thought about you." Then he was silent for a while. "Can you ever forgive me?"

"It's me who needs to ask your forgiveness. I wasn't much of a father. But you know now I want to be."

Jack said nothing, but looked at his father and then rushed back into his arms. They hugged each other and Jack whispered, "Can you do me one last favor, Dad?"

Jake wiped the tears off his cheek. "Another favor, son? I guess so."

"I want you to call me 'Little Jake' from now on."

*

"Melanie, I am going to call your mother now to tell her you're safe," Jake said and walked into the house. As soon as he opened the front door, the phone rang and the big Indian met him in the living room with telephone in hand. "It's for you, boss. It's Dr. Hayes. I told her Melanie is here and safe. She is plenty pissed off."

Jake lifted the phone and immediately recognized it was Jo Hayes. After he told her the children were home and he was about to call her, he was surprised at her response. There was a chill in the tone of her voice as if she was calling from the dark side of the moon.

"Jake, I really don't want to talk to you right now. I'll be over to pick up Melanie in a few minutes. Please have her ready." She hung up abruptly and left Jake holding the dead line.

*

Jake was standing on the front deck of the cottage when Jo Hayes pulled up. She got out of the car and they stood in the driveway while Melanie went into the house to put her things together.

"What seems to be the problem, Jo? Thank God the children are safe."

"We're driving to Boston tomorrow. My three-month contract on the Vineyard is about over and we're heading back to Mass General."

"I thought you were leaving at the end of the month."

"Things change," she replied abruptly.

"Yes," Jake said pensively and thought this might be the time to get into it. "You're leaving tomorrow? Are you leaving because of what happened to Melanie today or could it be something else?"

Jo's voice turned distant. "I think it's best."

"Does Jack know Melanie is leaving?"

"I don't think Melanie should see Jack anymore."

"Because they were out alone on the jet ski together? I gave them permission."

"Not to go out in the ocean and certainly not to satisfy Jack's teenage hormonal needs."

"I'm sure the whole thing was quite innocent."

"Maybe, but I think I'm in the best position to make that judgment as a mother. I allowed my daughter to go out with Jack because I trusted him. I trusted him to take care of her and use good judgment. I am not going to let it happen again."

Jake was stunned by her icy candor. He waited a long moment to reply. "I think there's something you haven't told me."

"About what?"

"About the real reason you're leaving now."

She looked at him peculiarly. "What are you getting at?"

"You know exactly. You lied to me. You threw me a red herring, sent me sailing off on the wrong tack. The only question is, why? Why did you want to make me think Hugh McGreggor had a heart attack?"

"I don't know what you're talking about."

"My guess is there was nothing about a heart attack in his hospital records. I would have spent my time tilting windmills while pushing your bogus information about the captain's heart attack. In the end, it would have all come crashing down on my head. Eventually, the Martha's Vineyard Steamship Authority would show the jury Captain McGreggor's hospital records. They would see he didn't have a heart attack and I would be left with egg on my face. Case lost."

"I'm not going to listen to this nonsense a moment longer. I'm going in to get my daughter."

Jack and Melanie stood at the corner of the deck listening to the heated conversation. Melanie came out of the shadows. "No, Mother," Melanie shouted, "I want to hear why you lied to Mr. Dellahunt."

"You come right down here, missy. We're leaving."

Jake took the keys out of the ignition. "Not until you tell us all why you lied about Hugh McGreggor's heart attack."

"I am going to call the police if you don't let us leave."

"You do that. This steamship case isn't just a little local case. It's a federal case. I will have the feds charge you with obstruction of justice, witness tampering, and conspiracy to suborn perjury."

Jo Hayes said nothing.

"Alright, let me tell you, then. I did some checking on you. You practiced medicine in New York ten years ago. You were married to a lawyer then. I don't have to tell you he was one of Steven Dichentis' law partners at Baker, Block and Benson. So tell me right now before I drop a dime, who really had the heart condition?"

Jo Hayes was silent for a moment and then said, "It was Bobby Nicholson, the helmsman in the wheelhouse. He had a history of heart disease and they wanted to cover it up. They are powerful people. Doctors are busy. I'm not home as much as I would like. They threatened a custody suit if I didn't tell you the captain had a heart attack. I am sorry, Jake. Really sorry."

Melanie Hayes ran down the steps. "How could you, Mother?"

Jake handed Jo the keys and opened the door for her. Melanie was sobbing as she sat in the car. Jo Hayes looked up at Jake. "If you can find it in your heart to forgive me, I would like you to call."

"I think it's easier if you just leave without any promise of tomorrows."

Jake walked onto the back deck where Jack was leaning on the dock railing. He put his arm around his son and held him closely while he spoke softly to him. Robert Paul stepped out of the kitchen and looked through the glass sliders as the boy hugged his father and cried.

A.J. CUSHNER

Chapter Four

Case of Murder

Long before Jake Dellahunt inherited the cottage on Martha's Vineyard, Judge Sam Mathews owned it. Bob Cottle had built the house for Judge Sam on three acres of land at the edge of a narrow salt water inlet for the exorbitant price of twenty-five hundred dollars. It was a time before "Judge Sam," as islanders eventually came to call him, was fitted for judicial robes and elevated to the bench. It was a time when he was just a young country lawyer, a bit green behind the ears, and when the beauty of the island took his breath away. He lived in his newly built home on Lake Tashmoo and traveled to work by ferry and automobile between courthouses on Martha's Vineyard to Nantucket, Hyannis and Barnstable on Cape Cod.

It was 1942 and the country was at war. Just about every able-bodied man between eighteen and thirty-five on the island had volunteered to serve. Sam Mathews had tried to enlist twice, first in the army and then the navy. They both turned him down. They exempted him from the draft because the government declared he provided essential legal services to the Cape and Islands' communities. He had to settle for patrolling beach roads and shores in case of invasion. He stood guard at Packer's Oil and Gas Storage tanks one night a week, armed with a standard issue M-1 Garand rifle with one clip of eight .30-06 caliber bullets and two spare 8-round magazines in his belt. He asked to do more and they handed him a flashlight, whistle and white air raid warden's helmet and appointed him Air Raid Warden on Cottage Road. There were no air raids. Still, he did his duty keeping the few houses on the road blacked out.

*

The *Vineyard Gazette* came out on Fridays. Anyone who wanted island news before Friday went to the coffee shop in front of the bowling alley where they served food and exchanged gossip. Sam made it a point to have breakfast at the bowling alley coffee shop where he picked up the local dirt and dished out a few newly minted business cards, ink hardly dried, and scored an occasional client.

"Did you hear about the German sub they spotted off South Beach last night?" Al Brackman asked Sam Mathews one chilly February morning at the bowling alley coffee shop.

Sam Mathews dug into his fried eggs. "Can't say I heard anything."

Brackman owned the dry goods store on Main Street, the real estate company, the bowling alley and the coffee shop. He was a spry, little man who loved daily tittle-tattle. "Those German subs are playing havoc with beachfront property prices, I tell ya."

"Why is that?"

"Who wants to buy a house on the beach where a bunch of saboteurs are going to land?"

"How do you know they're coming?"

"Say the German U-boats are sending light signals in Morse Code."

"I didn't think the Germans knew Morse Code."

Brackman fancied himself an expert on most subjects. "Course they do, Sam. It's universal. And they was sending Morse Code to someone on the beach last night."

"Really? You think there's a spy on the island." Sam laughed at the idea.

Al Brackman waggled his index finger at Sam. "Probably Old Man Miller. You know the one. Lives in the shack at the end of Germantown Road. Not far from where the U-boat was spotted sendin' signals. In Morse Code."

"Old Henry Miller? Everybody on the island knows him. He's just a harmless old man. Why would you think he was involved?"

"First place. His name isn't Henry Miller. It's Heinrich Meuller. Get it. He changed it when he showed up on the island."

"So what? He came here years before the war. The ferry boats were probably square riggers when Old Man Miller first set foot on the island."

"Maybe so, but why did he go to the trouble of disguising his name?"

"His name didn't seem to bother you when he shopped in your dry goods store."

"Them Germans are pretty damned clever, pretending to be loyal Americans, looking like us and just waiting for a chance to take over."

"He's not taking over. He once told me he filed his citizenship papers the year Franklin Roosevelt moved into the White House. That was in '33."

"Then tell me why he changed his name."

"Lots of people change their names when they come to this country."

"Yeah, like who?"

"Like everyone in Hollywood."

"What do yah mean?"

"You go to the movies don't you?"

"Sure."

"Edward G. changed his name from Manny Goldenberg and Cary Grant's real name is Archie Leach."

"Do you really think Edward G. and Cary Grant are gonna send messages to the Krauts? Who else is a German U-boat going to signal around here?" Brackman bellowed.

"Having a German name doesn't automatically make him Herman Goering. There are a couple of people living here with German names, like Jimmy Schmitt and Kurt Heinman."

"Jimmy and Kurt volunteered the day we went to war against the Krauts. Besides, they wasn't seen on the beach last night."

"You saw Old Man Miller on the beach last night?"

"Not me."

"Then who?"

"They ain't saying. Loose lips sink ships, you know."

"You mean some nameless phantom."

"No ghost. Miller was seen on the beach last night."

"So what if he were on the beach. Maybe he's a sleep walker or went swimming because he had insomnia."

Al Brackman laughed. "Swimming in the middle of winter? The New Bedford ice breaker's clearing ice in the Sound and old Heinne Meuller went swimming in the frozen ocean last night. With what? His ice skates."

"So you think the old geezer's a spy, who ran down the beach in the middle of the night and sent out a bunch of dots and dashes to a German sub? Got the Green Hornet Code Ring, does he? Probably sent away with a Wheaties box top. Must have ordered the German spy edition."

"You can make all the fun of me you want, Sam. But it ain't going to change a thing."

"You've got to stop drinking all that coffee, Al. It's making you nuts."

Just then, there came a tapping on the window. Sam turned around and saw his secretary, Minna Pure outside, dressed in a heavy woolen hat, muffler and fur-trimmed black coat, puffing clouds of misty breath onto the frozen coffee shop window. She was a woman in her forties with ivory white skin, marked with fading freckles, a large straight nose, and dyed honey blond hair. Sam motioned her to step inside. She opened the door and walked over to the counter where the two men were sitting.

"Good Morning, Miss Pure."

"Good Morning, Mr. Mathews and Mr. Brackman."

"Are you just going to work?"

"Gracious no. I have been in the office for an hour this morning. Lots of typing and filing to be done. We have so many quitclaim deeds to type these days. It seems like everyone on the island wants to sell their house," she explained. "The Macombers and the Petersons are just two of the people selling in West Chop and you cannot imagine the prices. . ."

Sam interrupted her. "Is there some reason you wanted to speak to me, Miss Pure?"

"Oh gracious, I almost forgot. I came downtown to look for you. You received an urgent long distance telephone call from Boston this morning."

"From whom?"

She looked at Al Brackman in a queer sort of way. "I'd rather not say right now."

"Will you excuse us, Al?" Sam asked and ushered Minna by her arm to the corner of the counter where they could be alone. They sat down on round chrome stools.

When she was sure they could not be overheard, she whispered, "Did you know they arrested Mr. Miller late last night?"

"Old Man Miller?"

"The very person."

"Did he call the office?"

"Good gracious, no. Mr. J. Thomas Bradford from the Massachusetts Bar Association called from Boston this morning. He asked if you would represent Mr. Miller. He mailed you five hundred dollars as a retainer."

"He wants me to represent Miller? That's surprising since I only met Bradford last summer at the Yacht Club Bar Association party."

"He said you made an impression on him and he wanted someone from the island to handle the defense."

Sam nodded. "He sent five hundred dollars. That's a lot of money. Must be a pretty serious matter. Did he say what they charged Miller with?"

"He didn't. But then Doc Parsons called this morning and said Sheriff McCarthy asked him to perform an autopsy. He said he didn't want to come out of retirement and wanted you to speak to the Sheriff."

"You're going a little too fast for me. Who died?"

"Oh, nobody died."

"Then why would the County Sheriff's Office ask Doctor Parsons to perform an autopsy if no one died?"

"Nobody died. Somebody was murdered last night."

"Murdered? Nobody gets murdered on Martha's Vineyard. Not since Addie Whitcomb pushed her husband down the town well and ruined the drinking water for five years. Who was murdered last night?"

"One of the beach patrolmen on South Beach supposedly caught him signaling a German submarine last night and there was fight. There's supposed to be a witness."

"Slow down, Miss Pure. Who was the 'him' that was supposed to be signaling the Germans?"

"Why, Mr. Miller, of course."

"You're saying Old Man Miller got into a fight and killed someone and the Sheriff asked Doc to come out of retirement to perform the autopsy."

"And there was a witness."

"Do we know the name of the witness?"

"Gracious, no. Something about the government's war powers and a matter of state security. It's all very hush-hush."

Sam shook his head. "Miller is as much of a threat to state security as a nun in a church."

"I'm sure he's a hundred percent red, white and blue, Mr. Mathews."

"Not if he had the hard luck to be born in Germany."

*

"I know why you're here, Sam. Just get back in your truck and go home," Sheriff Jack McCarthy got up from his office chair in the county jail and poured a cup of coffee out of a large silver thermos. "I suppose you want a cup, too."

"Wouldn't mind, Jack. At least tell me. What's the charge you're holding him on?"

McCarthy poured Sam another cup of coffee. "Hope you like it straight up, 'cause we don't have any sugar or cream."

Sam took the cup and sat down. "It's fine."

"How did you get involved in this case, Sam?"

"Bar Association referral."

"Ever try a murder case before?"

Sam took a deep breath. "Can't say I have," Sam replied and thought about interviewing his new client. "Of course, it would be helpful if I could talk to my client."

"Forget it. I have my instructions from the FBI."

"I hate to bring it up, but I'm sure you remember the old Sixth Amendment guarantees the right to counsel in criminal cases."

"They told me the Constitution only applies to Americans and Heinne Meuller don't sound like no American. Besides, the Special War Powers Act suspended suspected collaborators' rights, like they done to the Japs on the west coast."

"Can't suspend the Constitution, Jack. You can admire it and protect it, but you can't conveniently ignore it."

"Maybe so, but I got my orders."

Sam knew he was fighting a losing cause. "Alright, but at least tell me when he will be arraigned."

"Depends on what they squeeze out of him. Look, I can tell you they are taking him to Boston and he'll be back here first of the week for a court appearance. I'll call you when he's ready to go over to the courthouse. I can't do any more for you, counselor."

At first light the following morning, a squad of MP's put the German on a Coast Guard cutter waiting at the town dock in Edgartown. It took six hours for the cutter to arrive at the Boston Army Base in South Boston where old Mr. Miller was chained hand and foot and then questioned for nearly fifteen hours. In the end, deprived of food, water, a toilet and sleep, the old man was given a piece of paper to sign he neither understood nor read.

*

The whole island was abuzz with talk of Old Man Miller and the murder on South Beach. Everyone on the island had him convicted. They were only uncertain whether to have a firing squad finish him off or drag him up to the top of the Gay Head lighthouse and hang him. Most told Sam they were in favor of leaving the Nazi hanging to rot from the lighthouse, so sailors on U-boats would know what they had in store. When Sam suggested Miller was entitled to a fair trial, they agreed and then thought he ought to be hung right after the trial. The war had finally come to Martha's Vineyard and the enemy was a seventy year-old man.

Gossip was the principal entertainment on the island and Sam Mathews had garnered the spotlight. The news that he had agreed to defend the murdering "German traitor" spread like wildfire. By the time Sam left the Sheriff's office and drove over to Packer's Texaco, they wouldn't accept any of his gas coupons. Sam couldn't buy gasoline for his pickup, food at Cronig's Market or find a smiling face on the street. When Sam walked back into Al Brackman's Coffee Shop, people wouldn't talk to him. They wouldn't serve him. Al Brackman, who was part of the small Jewish community on the island, had felt the sting of prejudice himself when his family first settled on Martha's Vineyard in the thirties. He stood in front of Sam and told him the Nazis had killed his family. Then he ordered Sam to get the hell out of his restaurant and never set foot in it again.

Sam left the coffee shop and walked slowly through the frozen morning mist to the A&P where he bought a small carton of Hood's milk and a package of stale Sunshine Oatmeal Raisin Cookies. Making his way to his second floor office in the old stone bank building, he felt more alone than ever. He had neither a wife nor a family and his few friends on the island were mostly summer people. The office was deserted. Sam's secretary, Miss Pure had left a note under the door saying she took the day off because of the threatening phone calls.

From the moment he entered the office, his phone didn't stop ringing. Clients called and asked for their files. Some warned him to drop the case. Others called and simply hung up without saying a word. After an hour, he stopped answering the phone, closed shop and went home.

When he climbed the stairs to the cottage deck, he stopped and stared at the front door. A white swastika, dripping with fresh paint, was plastered across the door. A torn cardboard box hung from the doorknob. Sam looked at the large letters crayoned across the cardboard: "YOU STINKING TRAITOR."

Sam ripped the cardboard from the door, walked into the living room and picked up the phone to call the police. The line was dead. Just as he put the phone down, Sam heard a car slowly running over the gravel. He looked out the window just in time to catch a glimpse of an old pickup creeping by the front of the house. Sam could make out the image of one person driving down the road in a typical rust-bucket of an island pick-up, but it was too far away to see the driver's face. He took a few steps closer when the front end of a gun loomed from the truck window. Sam dove to the floor as a pair of flashes and two deafening blasts shattered the front windows. Tiny glass shards flew about the living room, piercing anything in their way like quills of a porcupine. All Sam heard as he lay on the floor bleeding was the sound of the pick-up roaring down Cottage Road. Then silence.

*

When Doc Parsons and Chief Shea from the Tisbury Police Department finished up and left that evening, Sam turned off the lights and stretched out on the living room couch, resting a shotgun next to him. As the hours slipped by, Sam's mind wandered in a world between consciousness and sleep. It was a fitful night, half in dream and half in waking, thinking about defending a man who had spent half his life living with the enemy.

Sam was certain his life was worth a hell of a lot more than the five hundred dollars the Bar Association was going to pay him. It wasn't the money that drew him to the case, although God knew he could certainly use it. It wasn't even a matter of guilt or innocence. Sam knew all about scapegoats. In bits and pieces of sleep, he dreamed of how his father found him complicit and sentenced him to a childhood of brutality after his mother had died from complications during his birth.

Now, the twenty-seven year-old, freshly-minted, raw recruit of a lawyer faced the government's juggernaut and, deep in his gut, he knew saving the old German was as futile and pointless as stepping in front of an oncoming locomotive.

*

Sam awoke early and was shaving in the bathroom when he heard a car coming up the driveway. He grabbed a towel and, while still wiping the shaving cream off his nose and ears, he ran into the living room, picked up the shotgun from the couch and pumped one of the shells into the receiver. He unlocked the safety, stood at the kitchen window and waited.

A rusty Dodge pick-up truck pulled up. Sam saw a boy in the back, balancing himself precariously over the tailgate, one leg dangling outside and the other firmly gripped to the inside. The pick-up stopped close to the back deck and a huge Wampanoag Indian stepped out from behind the wheel. Sam watched Amos

146

Paul, Chief of the Wampanoag Nation open the back of the pickup and slide off a fish smoker built from parts of a corroded car trunk. The big Indian dragged the hunk of metal onto the back deck followed by the boy, who busied himself cleaning bluefish and sea bass he took from an ice chest. He skewered the chunks of fish together onto sharpened hickory sticks. Chief Amos Paul placed the skewered fish in the smoker and, when Chief Amos appeared satisfied, he came to the door.

Sam carefully locked the safety on the shotgun, opened the receiver and walked onto the deck, carrying the gun over his shoulder. Sam always thought of himself as average size. As he approached the Indian, he marveled at a man who was twice his girth and nearly a foot taller. "Good Morning Chief," he bellowed.

Amos Paul looked at the shotgun. "Good you have a gun, Sam. Good for birds and shooting wild goats."

Sam extended his hand to greet the huge Wampanoag. Amos Paul took Sam's hand and buried his own hand half way up Sam's forearm.

"I didn't know there were wild goats on the island."

"There are no wild goats. But sometimes a neighbor's goat wonders into my yard and we shoot it. Tastes good, goat on a stick."

"Doesn't the owner complain about shooting his goat?"

"Under Wampanoag law, the owner of the goat can only complain to the Chief. I do not get many complaints."

Sam shook his head and laughed. "And who is this handsome youngster?"

"He is my son, Robert Paul. Nine years old, but he is very big for his age."

"As are you, Chief Amos."

The Chief did not smile. "Mmm. I heard there was trouble in your house last night, Sam Mathews," the huge Wampanoag continued as he piled the hickory shavings and wood chips into the smoker's bed, lit them and placed more skewers of fish on racks.

"I heard that many will not sell you food or gasoline so I brought you this smoked fish machine as a gift and I have twenty gallons of gasoline for you in the truck."

"You heard right and thank you for your fish and fish machine. I'll pay you for the gasoline."

"Mmm," the big Indian said, as was his custom when he did not want to respond. The Chief never minced his words. "If I were still a lawyer, I would not defend that German man."

"You were never a lawyer, Chief. You're the Wampanoag Law Giver."

"Same as a lawyer."

"You never went to law school and became a member of the bar. You were not a lawyer."

The Wampanoag Indian thought a moment. "You are right, Sam Mathews. I am not. I do not choose to be a lawyer because lawyers are old dogs. They are crooked like an old dog's hind legs and they bark without teeth."

"I seem to remember you calling this barking dog of a lawyer when you sold day-trippers, straight off the ferry, bus tickets for bus tours without any bus. Do you remember all the trouble you had with your five wives you conveniently forgot to divorce? Do you remember or should I go on?"

"Mmm. Do not remind me of my five wives."

"I could use your help."

"Is it about the German man?"

"Yes."

A wave of white smoke poured from the trunk of the old Ford smoker and the big Wampanoag closed the trunk and faced Sam. "Why would you travel this path? It can only lead to a cliff where you will fall to the rocks and perish."

"I am surprised you feel that way, Chief. That old German is hated as are many of your brothers and sisters. He's drowning in a sea of fear and prejudice. Everyone around here just wants to see him strung up."

"And what if the German man has killed another human being?"

"I don't know who witnessed the murder, where, how or when it was supposed to have happened. He doesn't have a chance. Do you remember a time when the Wampanoag on this island were never given a chance? Much of their land taken from them? Thrown into whaling ships and paid no wages for their work? Do you remember when there were neither schools for the children nor medicines for your people?"

The big Wampanoag nodded. "What would you have me do?"

"Just help me with the German's case for a while. There are many who want to kill this German along with me. The police are no help. I want you to move into my house to be my assistant."

"To be a lawyer?"

"No Chief, to watch my house, clean and cook and help me search for the truth about what happened on South Beach."

Amos Paul thought a moment. "It might be better Sam Mathews to take a Wampanoag woman. She will clean and cook for you. You will not sleep alone, even if you wish to. I know many who would come to your door."

Sam laughed. "Thanks, but I already have one woman in my life. I'm married to a lady holding a set of scales."

"Is this the same woman who cleans fish at John's Fish Market?"

"No, this is a majestic woman who holds the Scales of Justice. Look, I'll pay you fifteen dollars a week, room and board. What do you say?"

"Can I bring my son, Robert?"

Sam looked at the boy. If Chief Amos was going to work for Sam, he could see it was going to be a package deal. "Sure. You can both start by having Cottle's Lumber Yard replace the front windows. Oh, and please get rid of that swastika on my front door."

"It is an old Indian symbol, Sam Mathews. It is a sign of a spirit migration."

"Then please have it migrate somewhere else."

"We will go to Cottle's and buy a new front door. They will put it on your bill."

"Just buy a can of green paint and have the boy give the door two or three coats."

*

"The check from the Bar Association came in this morning, Mr. Mathews. Do you want me to deposit it?" Miss Pure asked.

"How much did they send?"

She took the check from the envelope and held it up. "Oh gracious, it's five hundred dollars, Mr. Mathews. Just like Mr. Bradford said. What do you want me to do with it?"

The moment of decision had come. Just then the phone rang. Sam looked at the terrified expression on his secretary's face and said, "I'll get it." He lifted the phone off the hook.

"Attorney Sam Mathews' office, Sam Mathews speaking."

Sam recognized the voice immediately. It was Sheriff Jack McCarthy over at the county lockup. "Your man is here. We will be taking him over for arraignment in about an hour."

"Thanks for calling, Jack. I'm leaving now."

Sam picked up his briefcase and headed for the office door. "I'll be in Edgartown at the County Jail to see Mr. Miller." Sam turned and opened the front door.

Miss Pure stood up and held the Bar Association check in the air. "What do you want me to do with this?"

Sam looked back at the check. He didn't have to decide about taking the case until he heard what his client had to say. "I think you better hang on to it until I get back."

*

When Sam reached Edgartown that morning, he learned the old German had been taken to the courthouse basement holding pen. Two Shore Patrolmen led Sam down a rickety set of spiral stairs to a dark cage where, in the dim light, he saw the silhouette of a man at the far end of the iron box. The guards left and only Sam and the outline of a man sitting on a wooden stool behind bars remained.

"Mr. Miller, is that you?"

The shadowy figure in the cage didn't move. As Sam's eyes adjusted to the darkness, he caught a first glimpse of the old man's grotesque face. "It's Sam, Sam Mathews. I am going to be your lawyer. Is that you, Mr. Miller?"

Sam guessed it would only be minutes before they brought Miller to court. "You know, they're accusing you of killing a Beach Patrolman when he caught you signaling a U-boat on South Beach. Were you on the beach?"

"I *vould* never, never help the Nazis. They make me ashamed to be German."

Sam repeated the question. "I need you to tell me. Were you on the beach the morning the Patrolman was shot?"

The old man didn't answer at first. He stood up. Then in a raspy whisper, Mr. Miller said, "*Ja,* Sam. I *vas* on the beach, but I swear to you I did not kill anyone. On my eternal soul, I swear I am innocent."

"What the hell were you doing on the beach in the middle of a freezing night?"

"Sometimes I cannot sleep. I walk near the water for a while. It's not far from my house."

"With a flashlight?"

The old man drew closer. "*Ja,* I had a light with me."

"To signal a German sub in Morse Code?"

"No, just to light the path in the woods."

"What did you tell the police?"

The prisoner dragged one leg across the cell until he reached the bars and stood in front of Sam. "*Vat* would you tell them to keep alive?"

Sam could see the old man plainly now. Bent over like a broken tree limb, his shoulders rounded, his face dark, flesh torn and hanging loosely, with red eyes disappearing into a pair of sunken sockets, he held out his trembling hands to Sam. Sam took and held them firmly. Then the old man began to cry.

"My God, what have they done to you?" Sam asked.

*

"Where's Judge Cahill, this morning?" Sam asked Marlin Fredericks. "I want him to remand my client to the hospital right away."

The Clerk of Court, Marlin Fredericks stood up from behind his oak desk and walked over to the counter where Sam handed him a hand-written *ex-parte* motion.

"Horace Cahill isn't the judge in your case, Sam. They brought over a special judge assigned from Boston, Judge Ethan Elliot."

"All right then, I would like to see Judge Elliot."

"You sure, Sam? I think you might want to wait on that."

"And why is that, Marlin?"

"Orders. He wants to go by the book and he's not taking any *ex-parte* hearings."

"I would like to see the docket file on Mr. Miller."

"Sorry Sam. It's been sealed by Judge Elliot."

"I thought we were going to have a real trial, not a dog and pony show. Am I missing something, Marlin?"

A deep and commanding voice responded from behind them. "It's the war, Sam. Didn't you know we're in a life and death struggle against the forces of fascism? It's a war against evil. That's why I'm here."

The voice reverberated around the large, open room and shook the very windows. If ever someone had the voice of God, it was J. Edward McCormack. Sam turned around to face the Attorney General of the Commonwealth of Massachusetts, a tall, handsome, gray-haired man with chiseled features. The former Harvard football star had followed in the footsteps of his late grandfather, U. S. Senator James Francis McCormack and now, the Attorney General, was the darling of the Massachusetts political machine.

Sam said nothing, but the sight of the Attorney General sent his mind spinning like torn scraps of paper caught in a tornado. Why would they bring in Eddie McCormack, a legendary courtroom veteran, to prosecute the case? Why would Massachusetts Bar Association hire a rookie like Sam to defend old man Miller? Why were they keeping their eye witness under wraps? Whether old man Miller killed someone or not, guilt or innocence didn't seem to matter. The answer was simple. The old German had to die.

Sam cleared his throat. "Brought in the heavy artillery for this one, did they Mr. McCormack?" He walked over to the A.G. and shook his hand.

"Sam, I'm here to prosecute your client and make sure justice is done."

"Mr. McCormack, how can justice be done when they beat a confession out of a seventy year-old man? How fair is it to seal the docket, to prevent counsel from interviewing the prosecution's key witnesses, to give the defendant a chance to see the evidence against him?"

"It's the War Powers Act, Sam. The WPA gives us the right to seal files and maintain the anonymity of witnesses. Your client will have his day in court. You'll hear all the evidence."

"What about the Constitution? You've trashed his rights guaranteed by the Constitution."

"It's 1942. Mr. Miller only has a right to counsel. The Sixth Amendment doesn't guarantee access to courthouse files and to interview witnesses. Sam, didn't you pay attention to your Constitutional Law course?"

"I sure did," Sam replied. "See you in court, Mr. McCormack."

*

With a dour, prune face attached to a chicken-boned, scrawny body, Judge Ethan Elliot looked old enough to have been around when the waters parted in the Red Sea. Lawyers around the Commonwealth still swore he sentenced the Salem witches to be burned alive at the stake. He was a mean, no-nonsense Puritan whose family came over on the Mayflower and had put more men in the "chair" than the entire furniture department at Filene's Department Store.

Judge Elliot pointed a boney finger at the Prosecutor and his faced nearly cracked when he tried to smile. "Ah, Mr. Attorney General, do you wish to begin with an opening statement to the jury?"

J. Edward McCormack was imperially flanked by two young Assistant AG's. He stood up seemingly to pose his athletic frame and good looks in front of the jury. Without responding to the judge, he faced the jury and replied, "No thank you, Your Honor. This is an open and shut case and we only have a handful of witnesses. So if I may . . ."

"Objection," Sam called out.

The judge squinted his two beady eyes at Sam. "What is the nature of your objection, young man?"

"Mr. McCormack's personal or professional assessment of this case is not proper."

"Overruled. Sit down and wait until the case begins before you begin making any objections," the thin-lipped judge warned dismissively with a hiss and then turned his attention to the Attorney General. In an inviting tone, dripping with honey, he purred, "Call your first witness, Mr. Attorney General."

Sam bit his lip, but sat down beside his client.

McCormack turned to face the courtroom and strutted past the jury, nodding to each of them, until he reached the end of the railing. "Call FBI Agent, Hans Kaufmann."

Kaufmann stood up and walked forward. He was a large man, but the first thing Sam noticed about Agent Kaufmann was his eyes. They were dark, almost black and surrounded by even darker circles, much like the bulls eye of targets. His mouth was twisted as if he had suffered some terrible shock that left his face distorted.

His cropped black hair stood on end as if held by a magnet. The clerk swore him in and he took a seat in the witness box.

McCormack moved to the back of the railing. "Are you employed, Mr. Kaufmann?"

"I am a German language translator for the Boston District of the FBI."

McCormack pointed to the old man sitting next to Sam. "Do you recognize the man sitting over there next to Attorney Mathews?"

The witness smiled malevolently. "*Ja,* I know *Herr* Miller."

"Under what circumstances to did you meet Mr. Miller?"

"They asked me to question *Herr* Miller after he *vas* arrested and brought to Boston."

"Did they tell you why they chose you to interview Mr. Miller?"

"*Ve* came from the same town in northern Germany and *ve* both spoke the same dialect of northern German."

"And what, if anything, did you find out?"

"Mr. Miller told me he *vas* an agent of Germany sent here many years ago. The man he killed caught him signaling a U–boat. He shot the man and ran up the dunes back to his house."

"Are you sure? Did Mr. Miller tell you he shot Joe deSilva?"

"He said he fired two shots and he signed a written confession."

"Did he tell you why he was willing to sign a confession?"

"*Herr* Miller told me he was proud of the Motherland and was not afraid to tell the truth."

McCormack walked over to the clerk's desk and picked up a piece of paper. "Is this the paper Mr. Miller signed?"

"Yes. He signed it in front of me."

McCormack returned the paper to the clerk and walked back to his seat. "No further questions."

Sam went directly to the clerk's desk, picked up the piece of paper and read the hand written confession. Then he handed it to the witness. Please read this aloud to the jury, *Herr* Kaufmann."

"Objection to calling an FBI Agent, '*Herr*.'"

The judge did not look up. He nodded and said, "Sustained."

Sam continued. "Alright, then instruct this witness to refrain from calling my client, '*Herr* Miller.' Mr. Miller is an American citizen with the right to be called, 'Mister Miller.'"

This time the judge looked up. "Do you have a question, Mr. Mathews?"

Sam turned his attention to the witness seated in the box. "Read the words on the paper in front of you to the jury."

Kaufmann picked up the statement. "'I, the undersigned Herman Miller confess I shot Joe de Silva on South Beach on the morning of February 14, 1942. (signed) Herman Miller.'"

Sam took the paper and studied it for a moment. Then he handed it back to the FBI Agent. "The confession is not the same handwriting as the signature."

"I wrote the statement and Miller signed it."

"I see. He refused to write out an admission of guilt in his own hand. How do we know it's his signature?"

"He signed it in front of me."

"Anyone else around?"

"No, just the two of us."

"So we're supposed to take your word for it."

"I am not lying."

"When you met, did you tell Mr. Miller you were an FBI agent or a friend from northern Germany?"

"I told him I *vas* an agent."

"Tell the truth. When you met, you never identified yourself as an FBI agent."

The agent hesitated and looked at Eddie McCormack. Sam knew he hit a nerve. "Perjury carries a heavy penalty in the Commonwealth. I ask you again. When you met, did you ever identify yourself as an FBI agent?"

"*Vell*, actually I did not right away."

"You let him believe you were just a fellow countryman."

Kaufmann lowered his head. "Yes."

"You lied to him. How do we know you're not lying about his signature?"

"I am telling the truth. He signed it."

Sam walked back to the defense table and opened a file. He removed a small piece of paper and held it up. "Really? I have a copy of Mr. Miller's signature on a canceled check. I want you to compare the two signatures." He slapped the check on the edge of the witness box. "Are the signatures on the check and the so called confession the same?"

Eddie McCormack jumped to his feet. "Objection."

"What is your objection, Mr. Attorney General?"

"This FBI agent is not an expert in handwriting."

Sam then turned to the judge. "I move we publish the signature of the so-called confession and the signature on the check to the jury and let them compare the two signatures."

"This might be a good time for the morning break." The judge dismissed the jury and waited for them to file out. He ordered the lawyers into chambers and asked the clerk to bring along the defendant's check and written confession. "Let me see the two signatures."

The judge took off his robes, sat down and put on his reading glasses. He shook his head and looked up at Eddie McCormack. "These two signatures are not the same. Any fool can see the signature on the check is different from the signature on the confession. As a matter of law, I cannot suppress the confession, but I will allow the jury to compare the two signatures and use their best judgment."

After the mid-morning break, the jury was called back and given the two signatures for comparison. Sam could see the question he planted in their minds after they had time to compare the two signatures. He had planned to ask Agent Kaufmann about the interrogation techniques, the handcuffs, leg irons, lack of food, water, toilet, and the cruelty, but thought he had gone far enough.

If he went further, he risked having the jury believe Kaufmann coerced his client into signing the confession and thus validate the old man's signature. In the end, Sam felt confident he had done enough to neutralize the confession.

The judge excused the witness and nodded to Eddie McCormack to call his next witness.

The Attorney General obliged and called Ray Shea, Tisbury Chief of Police. The clerk quickly swore in the Chief, who then took his seat in the witness box.

"Can you tell the jury where you were at approximately 7:00 o'clock on the morning of February 14, 1942?" McCormack began.

"I was summoned to South Beach."

"Is South Beach a part of your town of Tisbury?"

The chief looked at the jury. "Technically, it's out of my jurisdiction. But before I became Police Chief in Tisbury, I was the only state police certified homicide detective on-island. All of the six towns on Martha's Vineyard are short-handed so we often trade police resources. I was called to South Beach about 6:00 a.m. that morning to investigate the death of Auxiliary Beach Patrolman, Joe deSilva."

"When did you arrive?"

"About first light, at seven."

"Can you describe the scene?"

"Joe deSilva was lying on the beach in the sand, shot to death, face up, with his rifle still slung over his shoulder. On closer examination, I could see he had taken what looked to be two large caliber shots directly to the chest and shoulder area and bled out. A single pair of tracks ran up the dune from the place we found the body and disappeared in the woods toward Germantown Road."

"Germantown Road? Isn't that the road where the defendant, Mr. Miller lives?"

"That's why some of the people on-island refer to it as Germantown Road."

"Can you give us an approximation of the time of death?"

"From the warmth of the body and the lack of rigor, I would say around 3 or 4 a.m."

"Were you able to recover any bullets or bullet casings?"

"Joe was shot with a high velocity rifle while he was standing. The shots knocked him on his ass. They went right though him and are probably somewhere in the woods or buried in sand. We never found the shells or the casings."

"Who found the body?"

"Dick Chase, another Auxiliary Beach Patrolman who came to relieve Joe around 5:30 found his body. He immediately called the Beach Patrol Commander from one of the houses."

"Did you determine whether Mr. Miller owned a weapon?"

"We did at a later date."

"What did you learn?"

"Mr. Miller owned a thirty-ought-six Remington bolt action rifle that had been fired recently."

"In your experience, was the rifle Mr. Miller owned consistent with the kind of weapon used to kill Auxiliary Beach Patrolman deSilva?"

"Yes, it is the same type."

McCormack slowly returned to his seat. "I have no further questions."

The chief rose from his seat in the witness box and was about to step down when Sam jumped up. "Just a moment, please. I have some questions."

Sam moved from the defense table and stood in the well. He really wanted to ask Chief Shea how many times he had rehearsed his testimony with the prosecutors, but knew better. Instead, he asked permission to approach the witness and stopped a few feet in front of the witness box. "Chief," he began, "when you arrived at the scene of the shooting, did you determine whether the body had been moved at all?"

"I can assure you the body had not been moved. Nobody had touched the body."

Sam looked at his notes. "You testified Joe deSilva was lying face up, after – and I quote, 'he was shot with a high velocity rifle while he was standing. The shots knocked him on his ass.' Unquote. You concluded he was knocked backward from the force of the bullets. Is that correct?"

"That's what I said."

"Was the body lying on the beach or in the sand dunes above the beach?"

"It was lying on the beach about fifty feet down from the sand dunes."

"Which direction? Parallel to the ocean or were his feet toward the water and head toward the dunes?"

"The body was at a right angle to the ocean, his head toward the dunes and feet toward the water."

"Did you examine the wounds to see the entry and exit point of the bullets that presumably killed Joe deSilva?"

"Yes. They entered his shoulder and chest and exited his back."

"So, he was walking toward the ocean or facing the water when he was shot."

The chief thought a moment. "Yes, I guess that's true. He was shot facing the water. What the deuce are you getting at Sam?"

"I'll get to that in a minute. I have subpoenaed the Auxiliary Beach Patrol Commander, but perhaps you can tell us whether Mr. deSilva was assigned to walk along the beach or on the sand dune above the beach?"

"Along the sand dunes. It commands a better view of the beach," the Chief explained.

"But he came off the dunes to the beach before he was shot. Could the footprints you described actually be Joe deSilva's when he walked down the dune, onto the beach and toward the water?"

"It's possible, but the shoeprints seemed to go in the opposite direction from the beach to the dunes."

Sam ignored the answer. "I would put it to you that something in the water or just offshore attracted him. I would suggest he walked down the dune to investigate when someone either in the ocean or just offshore shot him twice."

McCormack stood up. "Objection, your honor. Calls for speculation."

Sam did not wait for the judge to rule. "You put him on the stand as the expert police homicide investigator."

The judge seemed annoyed, but said, "Restate your question, Mr. Mathews."

Sam moved in front of the witness. "Could something in the water or just offshore have caused the victim to leave his assigned path on the dune?"

"It's possible something or someone attracted him and he walked down to the beach to investigate. It's just as possible he went down to the beach to take a leak." Spectators laughed and stomped their feet and the judge threatened to clear the courtroom if there was another outburst.

Sam didn't like the answer, but showed no sign of it. "In the course of your investigation, did you learn whether Joe deSilva knew Mr. Miller?"

"He might have."

"'Might' doesn't count in the courthouse. Do you know if the decedent knew the defendant Miller?"

"No, I don't know whether they knew each other."

"Didn't you think it was important?"

"My job was to find the killer, not to see if they were pals."

"If Joe deSilva did *not* know Mr. Miller, can you tell the jury the reason he came off the dune with his rifle still shouldered?"

"Maybe he did know Miller."

"Didn't you just say you weren't aware deSilva and Mr. Miller knew one another?"

"Yes."

"Would it be fair to say deSilva came off the dune with his rifle remaining on his shoulder because he knew the person he was approaching?"

"Yes, I suppose that's true, but it didn't tie any one particular person to the crime."

"But wouldn't it pretty much exclude anyone that he did not know?"

"Yes, assuming he could see the person he knew when he came down from the dune."

"If an Auxiliary Beach Patrolman saw someone signaling a U-Boat, was he trained to take his weapon off his shoulder?"

"Absolutely."

"If he came down to the beach with his rifle still strapped to his shoulder, he was probably not approaching some spy signaling a Nazi boat in Morse Code?"

"If he saw something like that, he would have approached with his gun in hand and loaded."

"Before we get to *who* fired the shots, can you be certain the shots were fired from the direction of the water towards deSilva?"

"Yes."

"Did you send divers into the water to search for the shell casings?"

"No."

"Did you take Plaster of Paris casts of the footprints to see if they matched either the victim's or defendant's shoes?"

"No, by the time I arrived, the footprints were pretty much eroded and filled in because of the winter wind and all."

"When you asked Mr. Miller about his rifle, did he admit he owned it and give it to you immediately?"

"He did."

"Given meat rationing for the war effort, do you know how many people hunt deer during the winter months?"

"No, it's illegal. Out of season."

"You know people hunt deer on-island all year round."

"That's a fact, although it ain't legal," the chief replied to laughter in the gallery.

"Would you say the most popular deer rifle on this island is a 30-ought-6?

"Probably."

"Same as the rifle Mr. Miller owns, isn't it?"

"Yes."

"Would you agree more than a hundred people on-island shoot deer for venison?"

"Yes."

"Did you check to see if their guns were fired recently?"

"No."

"The shooting took place on a bitterly cold night, yet you testified from the warmth of the body and the lack of rigor, de Silva was killed between 3:00 and 4:00 a.m. The temperature was 15 degrees Fahrenheit according to the US Weather Service. If your estimates were correct, the body would have been frozen stiff by the time you arrived at 7:00 a.m. Was he killed closer to 5:00 a.m.?"

"No, I did consider the weather conditions when making my estimate of the time of death. He had dressed in double thermals. Body would have retained heat for a longer time. I gave you my best estimate."

"How many murders on this island have you investigated?"

"Come on, Sam. Nobody gets murdered on Martha's Vineyard. You know that."

"If that were true, we wouldn't be here." Sam looked up at the bench. "Judge, will you instruct the witness to answer?"

"Answer the question, Chief."

"This is my first murder case."

"Your first murder case," Sam repeated facing the jury. "If you don't have a credible confession, a murder weapon, ballistics, the brass shell casings, fibers, shoe molds, or any forensic evidence, what in the world are we doing here?"

J. Edward McCormack objected, but before the judge could rule, the witness blurted out, "We have an eye witness, who saw your client shoot Joe deSilva."

*

"Sam, what in the earth are you doing sittin' on my doorstep in the dark?" Al Brackman asked as he climbed up the front stairs to his house. "You look half frozen. How long have you been camped out on my porch? Come in and set yourself next to the stove."

Sam said nothing as he followed Al into the house. Al's wife, Sarah made tea while the two men moved to the back of the house into Al's office warmed by a woodstove. Sam took off his overcoat and gloves and stood warming his hands in front of the iron stove. Al sat in one of the brown leather chairs.

"You know Sam, I was in court for a while today."

"I thought I saw you, but there were so many people."

"You were nothin' short of masterful."

Sam shook his head and smiled.

"No, I really mean it. You got half the people on the island thinking they got the wrong man."

"I hope they're on the jury," Sam laughed.

"I know most of the people on that jury and they're a level-headed lot. You would have my vote today." Al opened the woodstove with a poker and threw in a couple of logs. They caught the heat and he stared into the flames. His words grew slow, almost as if they were buried in his throat and did not want to come out. "I'm awful sorry about the other day. Just got caught up in all them things those Nazis are doing. My wife says I shouldn't get excited. Bad for the ticker."

"You know someone took a pair of potshots at me."

"Heard all about it from Chief Shea."

"Does he have any idea who did it?"

Al Brackman snickered. "Chief is a good man, but he couldn't find a pie his mother baked if it was sittin' on her own kitchen table."

"Look Al, I could really use your help."

"My help? For what? Seems like you're doin' just fine."

"Their whole case rests on the testimony of one eye witness."

"Do you know who he is?"

"They've kept him under wraps from the very start."

"I see and you think I can help, do you?"

"If anyone on this island has any idea who he is, you'd be the person. Nothing gets by your grist mill."

"I'd like to help you, really."

"Anything at all that might help me to prepare."

"It would only be a rumor running around the coffee shop."

"You know something, don't you Al?"

Al shook his head. "Maybe and maybe you'd like to do some old-fashioned horse trading."

"What do you mean?"

"I'd like to know what Miller's got to say for himself. Did he tell you he killed Joe? What did he tell you?"

"You know I can't reveal anything a client tells me."

"You want to trade information. Here's your chance."

Sam knew if he said anything, Al would be serving it up with the breakfast special. He thought about losing his livelihood. "All I can tell you is he didn't kill deSilva."

"How do you know? Got an alibi, does he?"

"I didn't say that. I can tell you he hates the Nazis."

"Was he home sleeping? Is that his alibi?"

"He lives alone."

"So he doesn't have an alibi."

"I believe him."

"You're supposed to believe your client."

"What have you got for me, Al?"

Brackman thought about it for a moment.

"Come on Al, you don't want to see an innocent guy put in the chair."

Just then, Al's wife came in carrying a small tray with tea and cakes. She was a pretty dark haired woman with laughing eyes and a beautiful smile.

"How is your daughter doing, Mrs. Brackman?" Sam asked her.

"She's doing just fine, Sam. She is the smartest child in the first grade."

"Got your brains Sarah, thank God," Al said and laughed.

"I know you two are discussing something in private, so we'll talk later. Good luck Sam." She turned and walked back toward the sewing room.

Brackman shook his head, but said nothing. Sam sipped his sweet tea and waited.

"OK, you never heard this from me," Al leaned over and whispered, "Check out the Harbor Master's shack in Menemsha, Manny Amaral's place."

"Manny Amaral?"

"People are sayin' he's been out on his boat all hours of the night and on the south side of the island. I ask you, what's the Harbor Master of Menemsha doing on South Beach in Gay Head at 4:00 in the morning, running around in an outboard? Something fishy if you ask me and Manny Amaral ain't likely running a boat off the beach to catch no sea bass. Check out that shack, Sam." Al tilted his cup and finished his tea. "Now, I ain't saying another word." With that, the small man set the cup down on the table next to his chair.

Sam stood up and walked over to Al. "You may not be saying another word, but by God you're coming with us tonight, if I have to kidnap you."

*

When Sam arrived at the cottage on Lake Tashmoo that evening, he found Chief Amos Paul sitting on the living room couch, glued to a wooden radio completely captivated by a half-hour broadcast of the Lone Ranger. Sam said nothing, took off his gloves and overcoat and sat down at the writing desk in front of a portable Smith-Corona where he began typing.

At the General Mills commercial break, Amos Paul turned to Sam. "Which do you like better, Tonto or Lone Ranger? I bet you like the white man better."

"I like them equally."

"I think the Indian is better. He is always saving the masked man."

"Yes, I'm sure," Sam replied.

Amos Paul thought a moment. "We are like them. Can I call you Kimosabe?"

"Amos, please. I'm trying to type these papers for court tomorrow morning."

Then the Indian asked, "What are you typing?"

"It's a paper asking the judge to make the government's secret witness produce any weapons he owns before he testifies."

"Mmm. But for what reason will they not let you see this witness?"

"I don't know," Sam said. "Maybe they think he'll let something drop that would crack the case wide open."

The big Wampanoag thought a moment and replied. "You mean like when the morning sun tells the ocean fog to leave and the land appears."

"Yes, but in this particular case, Mr. McCormack thinks he's going to lift the fog."

"Mmm," the big Indian murmured as the "Cereal of Champions" commercial ended and he returned to his program.

"What do you know about the Harbor Master in Menemsha, Manny Amaral?"

"Manny? I think he has a couple of boys in the Air Force."

"But what do you know about him?" Sam asked several times without any reply.

Finally, Amos Paul looked away from the radio and responded. "This is the best part. They have the Lone Ranger surrounded and

Tonto is going to have to rescue him once again. It will soon be over."

Sam shook his head and continued typing.

*

A winter moon as pale and yellow as a cadaver hung over the shacks along Menemsha Creek that night. Sam slowed his truck to a crawl as they approached a row of shacks on a narrow ocean inlet.

"It's the second one over there," Al Brackman whispered to Sam, pointing to a weather-beaten shingled Cape with its backside standing on stilts. A pier ran downward from the back of the house to a floating dock, where a skiff with an outboard motor bobbed up and down in the creek as it tried to join the outgoing tide.

Sam stopped and parked at the end of the creek. The three of them stayed seated inside for a moment. Amos Paul rolled down the window and stuck out his head. "Manny Amaral's boat is on the dock. Maybe he is inside his lodge."

"Shhh, you're going to wake up the dead," Sam whispered to the chief, holding his index finger to his lips.

"I don't see Manny's old Chevy around," Al Brackman observed. "I'll stay here and watch the truck while you two boys check out the place."

"The hell you are," Sam whispered. "This was your idea from the beginning and you're coming with us."

Sam and Amos opened their doors and stepped into the frigid night air. Al hesitated momentarily, but saw the big Indian watching him. Cautious as a feral cat, Al reluctantly crept out of the truck and quickly joined them. They walked quietly along the dirt road until they reached the shack and then crept up the stairs to the small front porch. Sam looked into the darkness behind the front windows. He turned on his flashlight and the held it against the window for a moment.

"Well what do you see?" Al asked after a few seconds.

"Nothing. Looks empty to me."

Sam tried turning the doorknob. It was locked. The big Indian walked over to the door and leaned his huge shoulder on it. The frame splintered and the door flew open. Amos stepped into the shack and Sam pushed Al into the blackness.

Sam pointed his Eveready, four-battery, warden's flashlight at an array of wires and followed them to a table where a large, gray metal radio sat next to a pair of earphones.

"Christ, it's a shortwave radio," Al exclaimed. "What's Amaral doing with a shortwave radio?"

"What is that over there on the wall?" Amos Paul asked.

Sam pointed the flashlight at the object.

"It's a gun."

"A rifle."

"Never saw one that long before."

Al Brackman lifted the rusted, old, bolt-action rifle off the wall. "Shine your light over here, Sam." Al examined the gun closely. "I've seen this kind of weapon before. A lot of the doughboys brought home Mausers from the First Big One for souvenirs. It's German alright. Look at the stamp, *'Gemacht in Deustchland.'* That means, made in Germany. "

"There is a box of bullets on the shelf," added the Chief.

"Are the shells all there?" Sam asked as he turned the beam of light on the small cardboard box of bullets the chief was holding.

"No, some are missing."

"How many?"

"I will have to count them," Chief Amos replied.

Al was still looking at the rifle. "Do you think Amaral shot Joe deSilva with this Mauser? It's pretty rusty. Probably hasn't been used in thirty years." Al swung the bolt around and opened the chamber. "I think it still works. What do you want to do with it?"

"Put it back like you found it."

The Indian picked up a small, framed photo of two boys, who were dressed in Army Air Force uniforms. "Who are these boys in this picture?"

Just then the headlights of a car filled the room for a second. Sam turned off the flashlight and room went black. The three men moved to the front window and watched a Chevy drive by the shack slowly and stop. A thin, bald man with broad shoulders and a hawk-nose stepped out of the old car and walked toward the shack. In the pale moonlight, there was no mistaking Manny Amaral.

"We're sure going to get into a heap of trouble for this," Al Brackman whispered.

"Oh, shut up, Al," Sam and Amos replied in unison.

The three of them stood behind the front door waiting. They listened to the footsteps moving up the front stairs and then around the porch to the pier. They quietly moved to the back window and watched Manny in the moonlight. He stepped into his skiff. The deafening roar of the old Evinrude outboard on the stern of the skiff shook the shack as the boat moved down the creek towards the ocean. Sam looked at the luminescent dials of his watch. It was close to 3:00 a.m.

*

When the jury was finally seated that morning, Judge Ethan Elliot addressed them with a paper-thin smile. "I apologize for keeping you in the jury room most of the morning, but we had some lawyer business before we could continue," he explained and then turned to the prosecutor. "Call your next witness, Mr. Attorney General," the judge said.

"Call the Menemsha Harbor Master, Chief Petty Officer Manny Amaral," Eddie McCormack responded.

Manny Amaral, middle-aged, but still muscular, dressed in Navy Whites with a colorful show of medals and ribbons pinned in neat rows to a spotless jacket, stood up from the throng of spectators sitting in the back of the courtroom and came forward. He was sworn and took his seat in the witness chair. He hardly looked like the person Sam had seen earlier that morning in Menemsha.

"Tell the jury about yourself," Eddie McCormack asked. "Where were you born, went to school and what jobs have you held?"

Manny looked at the jury. "Well, most of you know me. My name is Manuel Sol Amaral. I am forty-nine years-old. I was born right here on Martha's Vineyard. I went to school here, played baseball, basketball and football at All Island High School. I was captain of all three teams my senior year. When I graduated, I went off-island to Bridgewater State to study physical education. I left college after my first year to help work in our family's fishing business. The First World War came along and I joined the Navy where I first served on an ocean-going destroyer escorting the troops overseas and then in Naval Intelligence as a Portuguese translator. After the war, I stayed on, did twenty more and was honorably discharged in 1938 with the rank of Chief Petty Officer. Since leaving the Navy, I have worked for the town of Menemsha as Harbor Master."

McCormack had dressed Amaral perfectly to fit the naval hero theme. It was an Academy Award winning production and the State's Attorney General wasn't about to quit. He stepped out from behind the prosecutor's table and approached the witness. "I want to thank you for your service to the country as does every loyal American in this courtroom, *Petty Officer* Amaral. Do you hold any medals or special awards from the Navy?"

The witness pointed to the medals and fruit salad hanging on his chest. "This here on top is the Navy Cross, next to the Navy Distinguished Service Medal, Navy Commendation Medal, Navy Achievement Medal, and Navy Expeditionary Forces Medal. These ribbons underneath," he pointed out, "are awards for a Navy Presidential Unit Citation, Navy Unit Commendation, a Navy "E" Ribbon, the Navy Meritorious Service Commendation, the Navy Combat Action Ribbon, the Navy Overseas Service Ribbon, a Sea Deployment Ribbon, the Navy Rifle Marksman Ribbon, the Navy

Sea Service Ribbon, and the Navy Instructor and Language Ribbon."

"Did you get them all or leave some medals for anyone else?" McCormack quipped.

The spectators laughed and then rose and delivered a standing ovation. If Eddie McCormack wanted his witness to be a war hero, he had certainly succeeded.

The judge hammered his gavel. "I think that will be enough. Take your seats, ladies and gentlemen, and settle down or I will order the courtroom cleared."

After the gallery quieted, Sam stood up. "If it pleases the court."

The judge turned to Sam from the bench. "Yes, Mr. Mathews, do you have an objection?"

"I object to Mr. McCormack parading this witness around like the Prince of Wales. He is currently an ordinary American citizen, the Harbor Master for the town of Menemsha. The recitation we just witnessed of medals and awards, while admirable, is highly prejudicial."

McCormack was quick to counter. "His military service goes to the credibility of the witness, Your Honor."

"I agree, Mr. Attorney General. Objection denied. Please proceed with your direct examination, but you will no longer refer to this witness as, '*Petty Officer* Amaral.' He is to be called, '*Mister* Amaral.' Do you understand?"

"Yes, Your Honor."

Sam took his seat, but he knew the damage had been done.

Eddie McCormack continued, intentionally emphasizing the word, '*Mister*,' lest the jury forget the witness was a genuine war hero. "*Mister* Amaral, do you have any duties outside of your normal job as Harbor Master for the Town of Menemsha?"

"Yes sir. I also work for the United States Naval Intelligence Agency."

The words fell like a hammer on glass, shattering any theories Sam had considered about Amaral. The courtroom instantly fell as quiet as dust.

"Exactly what is your assignment, *Mister* Amaral? What is it that you do for Naval Intelligence?"

"German subs have been seen running off of the Vineyard and Long Island. They go deep during the daytime and come up to take in air and recharge their batteries at night. Intelligence has reason to believe the enemy may land saboteurs on our soil. My job is to look for any signs of U-boats."

"And how do you go about finding evidence of U-boats, *Mister* Amaral?"

"Look for an oil spill in the water, check the shoreline for washed-up garbage, see if they are signaling anyone onshore and listen to shortwave transmissions. That kind of thing."

Eddie McCormack stopped and looked at the jury. They clung to the witness' every word, every syllable as if imagining they were on South Beach with the war hero searching for U-boats.

"Where were you at approximately 4:00 a.m. on February 14th of this year?"

"I was in my skiff running close to the shore of South Beach."

"Did you see anything unusual?"

"I saw lights offshore signaling in Morse Code. I took out my binoculars and saw the silhouette of a German submarine. Then I saw someone standing right on the water's edge, sending signals back to the sub. When I got a few hundred feet away, I stopped my outboard and quietly rowed closer to see who was sending the signals."

"Did you recognize anyone?"

"It was Miller, Herman Miller. I had seen him around and recognized him."

"Are you sure?"

"I had the binoculars on him. There's no question it was him."

"But it was dark?"

"A full winter moon and stars were out."

"Can you point out the man you saw that night to the jury?"

"Yes, he's sitting over there next to his lawyer, Sam Mathews."

"What happened next?"

"Someone came down from the dunes. Miller turned around, picked up a rifle and I heard two shots. The man fell and Miller ran up the dunes and disappeared into the woods. I pulled my skiff into shore and ran over to help the man. It was Joe deSilva. He was unconscious. There wasn't anything I could do for him. He died within a few minutes."

"I have no further questions," Eddie McCormack said as he sat down. He turned to Sam. "You may inquire."

The judge banged his gavel on the bench and stood up. "We will adjourn until 2:00 p.m. this afternoon for cross examination if that is acceptable to you, Mr. Mathews."

*

"Now it all fits perfectly, the German Mauser rifle, the shortwave radio, the late night jaunts around South Beach," Al Brackman explained to Sam as they grabbed a sandwich at the Coffee Shop.

"A little too neatly for me," Sam replied.

"For crying-out-loud, Manny was working for the Navy Department. He sees a Nazi sub."

"No, he sees the silhouette of a U-boat," Sam corrected Al.

"Alright, but your man's signaling the boat and deSilva catches him. So Miller shoots Joe. There's the motive. It's open and shut."

"Convenient coincidence Petty Officer Manny is at the right spot on a beach seven miles long in the middle of a freezing winter night."

"You sayin' he wasn't there and didn't see nothing? He made it all up?"

"I'm saying it's all too neat. If it happened that way, why did Eddie McCormack dress Amaral in a sailor suit and run up the old red, white and blue?"

"I watched the jury. They believe him."

"Why the overkill? What are they hiding?"

"Sam, the guy wasn't hiding nothing. He's a hero through and through. One hundred percent, red-blooded American. I don't see how you can possibly win this case."

The tiny wrinkles on Sam's forehead were knotted tightly as tied shoelaces. "I'm sorry Al, but it all just seems too perfect for me. The old Mauser still works, a box of shells with missing bullets, the shortwave radio, three people on the beach and only one set of footprints in the sand, Popeye-the-Sailor-Man who doesn't call the cops, the body still warm three hours later, nobody hears his outboard that could wake the dead ten miles away and he doesn't go running after the killer." Sam scratched his head. "Does that add up to you?"

"Maybe yes and maybe no."

Sam smiled. "And that's what we lawyers call reasonable doubt."

*

The judge turned to the witness. "I remind you, Mr. Amaral, you are still under oath." Then he nodded to Sam to start his cross-examination.

Sam looked at the witness as he reached into his briefcase and pulled out the box of shells Chief Amos Paul had found in the shack. Chief Petty Officer Amaral saw the box of shells and, for a moment, Sam thought he saw the retired Naval Officer's appearance of smug confidence replaced with a look of fear. He placed the small box of cartridges on the defense table in clear sight of the jury and said nothing. Every person on the jury stared at the cardboard box, wondering what it had to do with the case.

The judge anxiously repeated, "It's your turn, young man."

Sam stood up and put his hands on the railing behind him. He said nothing as if collecting his thoughts before he began. "We've not had the opportunity before to talk about your testimony, have we, sir?"

"No, we have not."

"Did you ever come to know your identity was withheld from me and kept secret?

McCormack did not rise from his seat as he offered, "Objection."

"Sustained," the judge replied.

"Perhaps you can tell the jury, how many times you have spoken to the prosecutors about your testimony."

"I don't know. I never counted."

"More than six times?"

"Objection, the question has been asked and answered." The words slithered out of McCormack's mouth.

"Sustained. Move on, Mr. Mathews."

"Were you armed with a pistol or a rifle when you saw the defendant on the beach?"

"No, sir."

"Was it your practice to go out looking for saboteurs while unarmed?"

"Yes."

"Do you have a rifle or other firearm in your home or in your Harbor Master's shack?"

"No, sir."

"Mr. Amaral, I'm sure there are a dozen people in this courtroom who have seen a rifle hanging on the wall of your Harbor Master's shack in Menemsha."

"Oh, I have a World War One souvenir I brought back, but it's all rusted out."

"Really? I filed a motion earlier this morning and the court issued a bench warrant to bring in the weapon to show the jury," Sam said, moving to the bailiff's table and, lifting the Mauser from a covering, he pulled back the bolt and opened the chamber.

"It's still working, isn't it sir."

"I guess it may."

Sam handed the weapon to the witness. "Can you tell us where the rifle was manufactured?"

Amaral looked at the writing on the barrel. "It's in German."

Sam sarcastically mimicked the witness' earlier testimony. "But you have the Navy's Language Medal." Then Sam demanded, "Translate it."

Amaral did not hesitate. "It says it was made in Germany."

"Read the caliber of shells it takes?"

"It says 8x57 millimeter."

"Read the model number."

"K-98."

"According to the research I did at the Edgartown library this morning, K-98 Mausers were not manufactured before 1935, making it impossible for the gun to be a souvenir of the First World War."

"Maybe it was an experimental model. The Germans were always bringing new weapons into the trenches."

With the judge's permission, Sam picked up the rifle and gave it to the jury to inspect. Then he returned to the defense table and picked up the box of shells. He set them down on the edge of the witness box. "Do you recognize these?"

"No."

"Are you saying you do not have a box of shells in your shack?"

"Yes, but I don't know if that box of shells is the same," Amaral replied and examined it for a long while.

"So is the box yours?"

"No. It's not."

"What caliber are these shells?"

"It says, '8x57 millimeter.'"

"Isn't that the size your German rifle takes?"

"Yes."

"Is that a different size shell than the cartridges used in Mr. Miller's .30-06 Remington?"

This time, McCormack was on his feet. "Objection, Your Honor. Mister Amaral is not a ballistics expert."

"The witness testified he won the Navy Rifle Marksman Medal. I would think that qualifies him to know about the caliber of his own rifle and the most commonly used caliber deer gun on the island."

"Answer the question, if you know," the judge ordered.

Manny Amaral's face seemed strained as he turned toward the judge. "They are two different size bullets, judge. The .30-06 Springfield cartridge is taller and narrower than the shorter and wider 8x57 millimeter Mauser, but they are both rimless bottlenecked rifle cartridges."

"And using the words of Chief Shea, can the bullets from either Mr. Miller's .30-06 Springfield or your 8x57 millimeter Mauser 'knock you on your ass?'"

"Yes, if it were a chest shot. I suppose that's true."

Eddie McCormack had enough. "May we have a short recess, Your Honor?"

"The court will take a brief mid-afternoon recess."

*

When the courtroom cleared, the Attorney General asked Sam to join him in the small conference room off the vestibule.

"Sam, we've got a problem," Eddie McCormack began when they were alone. "I know how you found out about Amaral, his Mauser and the box of 8x57 millimeter cartridges. If you keep going down this road, we are going to move to strike your cross-examination, suppress the gun and shell evidence because of your unlawful search and, after the trial, we'll charge you with breaking and entering, burglary of a dwelling house and obstruction of justice. You've broken every rule in the book and, at the very least, you're probably going to lose your license to practice law."

Sam wondered who ratted him out. He was sure it wasn't the Chief. Chief Amos Paul could do hard time standing on his head and Al Brackman was as tough as they came. "What do you want?"

"Change your plea to guilty and we'll forget about your little peccadillo last night. You won't do any jail time and you'll keep practicing law."

Sam didn't blink. "You haven't got shit, Mr. Attorney General. The whole island knows someone broke into Amaral's shack. You just don't know the-who-done-it part, do you?"

"Those bullets you paraded around the courtroom tell us who broke in and took them."

Sam breathed a sigh of relief. McCormack only had the box of bullets to connect him to the shack. "First of all, your witness denied under oath the box of shells was his. You're not going to get around that sworn testimony unless you want to call him a liar and cite the son-of-a-bitch for perjury. Second of all, you're an outsider on this island. You have no idea how many times people break into those shacks along the creek every week. So take your plea offer and shove it."

"Alright, then change your plea to guilty and we'll take the death penalty off the table. That's my final offer."

Sam nodded and thought a moment. Then he said, "If we lose, this case is going up to the Supreme Court on the inability to present a cogent defense because you withheld the identity of the key witness. We're going to make some law here."

"So that's your final word, Sam. You're not going to discuss the offer with your client and let him make the decision."

"I've had that conversation with my client already. Miller told me he'd rather fry in the hot seat before he admits to being a traitor and a murderer."

"Sam, you're underestimating the mood of the country and this jury. You're swimming in some dangerous waters."

"Eddie, I think we both know who really killed Joe deSilva and I think I know why."

*

179

The judge pointed to the clock on the wall. "We will continue until 5:00 o'clock or earlier if you finish with your cross-examination, Mr. Mathews." Then he turned to Manny Amaral, who was seated in the first row of the gallery. "Mr. Amaral, please resume your seat in the witness chair and remember you are still under oath."

Sam went to the end of the jury box with his notes in hand. "Let's continue where we left off. You testified you were in your skiff running close to the shore when you saw lights offshore signaling in Morse Code. You said you took out your binoculars and saw the silhouette of a German submarine. Then you saw someone on the water's edge, sending signals back to the sub."

The judge interrupted. "Is there some question there, Mr. Mathews?"

"Yes, Your Honor," Sam replied and returned to the witness. "As a Naval Intelligence Officer, do you know Morse Code?"

"Sure."

"What were they saying to each other?"

For the first time, Sam's question left Manny Amaral speechless.

"Do you want me to repeat the question?"

"No. I don't know what they were signaling one another because I was more interested in identifying the spy on the beach."

"You were assigned to look for subs that might land saboteurs, but you did not read the Morse Code transmissions between a Uboat and an alleged spy. Is that your testimony?"

"Yes."

"You testified when you were a few hundred feet away, you stopped your outboard and quietly rowed closer to see who was sending the signals. Would you agree your outboard motor makes one hell of a racket?"

"I don't know. No more than any outboard."

"You had a tailing south wind that night and you're saying the racket of the outboard could not be heard or alerted anyone onshore two hundred feet away?"

"Maybe I was three or four hundred feet away."

"So you are not sure how far away you were from the figures on the beach when you turned off your engine."

"No, not really."

"Is that because it was dark and distances were hard to estimate over water?"

"Yes, that's true."

"After you stopped the engine, how far did you row the boat?"

"Close enough to see it was Miller, Herman Miller."

"Through your binoculars."

"Yes."

"Hundreds of feet away."

"Maybe less."

"At 4:00 in the morning in the dark."

"Like I said, there was bright moonlight and all the stars were out."

"You couldn't estimate the distance from him when you shut down your engine because of the darkness, but now you would have us believe you saw him clearly?"

"I rowed closer to him."

Sam realized he was not making progress and changed the line of questioning. "Would it be fair to say you were working for Naval Intelligence to root out saboteurs?"

The witness thought a minute and then answered, "Yes and to look for any sign of a U-boat that might land them."

"But after the shooting, you didn't take off after the spy who was signaling the U-boat."

"No, I didn't have to. I knew it was Miller."

"Because you had seen him around?"

"Yes."

"When did you last see him around before the shooting?"

"I really can't say."

"Alright then, where was it you last saw him around?"

"I don't know the exact place. I can't tell you that either."

"Did you call the police after the shooting?"

"No."

"What did you do?"

"I returned to my boat and continued to look for the U-boat Miller was signaling."

"You didn't think it was important to call the police?"

"I figured an Auxiliary Beach Patrol would find his body and I couldn't really do anything more for Joe."

"Did you find any signs of a U-boat?"

"No."

"Maybe you can tell us why nobody found your footprints in the sand if you got out of your boat, like you say, and ran over to Joe?"

"Maybe the tide washed them away."

"Along with Mr. Miller's .30-06 brass cartridges?"

"Maybe."

"Wouldn't be your 8x57 millimeter Mauser brass they will find in the water?"

"Objection."

"Sustained."

"Did you see Miller pick up his brass casings after you allege he shot Joe deSilva?"

"No."

"Did you pick up any casings?"

"No."

"If the defendant shot Joe deSilva as you told us, can you explain how the brass on the beach seems to have disappeared?"

"I can't. Maybe they didn't look hard enough."

Sam walked to the defense table and pointed at the box of shells. "Did you take your Mauser rifle and this box of shells on your boat that night?"

"I told you that isn't my box of shells."

"There are two shells missing out of this box."

"Objection. Unless Mr. Mathews can lay a foundation the shells are Mr. Amaral's, the question is irrelevant."

The judge looked at Sam. "Can you connect those shells to this witness?"

Sam continued without answering. "You omitted telling the jury about your two sons, didn't you?"

Eddie McCormack jumped to his feet. "Objection, will the court rule on my first objection?"

Sam didn't give the judge time to respond. "Your two sons were killed in bombing raids over Europe, weren't they?"

The witness buried his head in his arms.

"They were shot down over France. The Germans killed them."

Manny Amaral's face turned red. He stood up and began waving his arms and swearing at Sam.

"You son-of-a-bitch. My boys died defending this country and you're not going use them to help that rotten traitor." Amaral tried to get off the stand to get to Sam. "You bastard, I'm going to get you for this."

The bailiff ran over and pinned Amaral in the witness chair.

"Like you tried to get Mr. Miller, but you missed, didn't you?"

"Sit down, Mr. Amaral," the judge barked. "Right now."

Sam began to shout. "You hate Germans. They killed your two boys. You hate all Germans. Miller is the enemy. Tell the truth."

"Objection."

"This is your last warning, Mathews," the judge was seething.

Sam paid no attention to him. He kept pushing. "That's why you tried to shoot Mr. Miller. It was dark, you were in the water and couldn't get a clean shot."

"Objection."

The judge was infuriated. "That's enough, your examination is over." He hammered his gavel and ordered Sam to sit down.

Sam could not help himself. "You missed the old German and hit Joe deSilva. Isn't that what really happened?"

Amaral sat in the witness box, fists clenched and sobbing.

"Move for a mistrial, judge," McCormack said in a controlled voice.

The judge hammered his gavel. "I am declaring a mistrial. You are in contempt of court, Mr. Mathews. The bailiff will remove you from this court until further order. The jury is excused from additional duty and I hereby order a new trial as soon as the defendant has an opportunity to obtain another lawyer."

*

For the next few weeks, Sam cooled his heels in the county lockup while Dean Pritchard took over as defense lawyer. The second trial lasted only four days and it took the jury less than ten minutes to come back with a verdict of guilty. Herman Miller was executed three days later after the Supreme Court refused to hear an appeal. When it was all over, they released Sam from jail.

*

Only Al and his cook were in the coffee shop in front of the bowling alley when Sam walked in. Al brought over coffee and some pie. "On the house, barrister. When did they spring yah?"

"A few days ago."

"You were doing pretty good there in court, until you went nuts and accused Manny of the killing," Al said. "Now the whole island is ready to put you in the chair like they done to Miller."

"The old man didn't do it, Al."

"That's not what the jury said."

"I know."

"You know the new lawyer, Mr. Pritchard, put Miller on the stand. That was a mistake. The German admitted he was on the beach with a flashlight. He swore on a stack of bibles he wasn't signaling no submarine, just out for a little stroll on the beach. Said he couldn't sleep. 'Course nobody believed him."

"I heard."

"So what are you going to do now?"

"My law practice is washed up. Nobody would hire me to fix a parking ticket around here."

"For sure. So what are your plans? Going into the clam diggin' business, are yah?"

"The Judge Advocate's Office is always looking for lawyers. The thought of leaving this beautiful island I love . . ." Sam's voice softened. There were tears in his eyes.

"Look at the bright side. You still got your license to practice."

"Yeah, it was close. The Mass Bar sent me a letter of reprimand. Nothing in it about taking my ticket."

"That's good."

Sam finished the coffee and pie and got up. "Al, thanks for your help. It just didn't turn out the right way. Maybe if we left the box of Mauser shells in the shack, Henry Miller would still be alive."

"Maybe is a sorry word, kid. I don't think it would have mattered. The island went to war against you and Miller. You're lucky to be breathing."

Sam nodded and walked out of the coffee shop. The next day, he handed the keys to his idyllic cottage on Lake Tashmoo to Chief Amos Paul and left the island.

*

"You have a telephone call from the States, Captain Mathews," the Sergeant said through the intercom.

"Put the call through."

The telephone rang. Sam picked it up. "First Corps, Judge Advocate General's Office, Berlin. Captain Sam Mathews speaking, sir."

"Sam, Sam Mathews?" a woman asked.

"Yes, this is Sam."

"Please hold for the newsroom."

Sam waited a few seconds and heard a voice crackling with static. "Mr. Mathews, I heard you were stationed in Germany and we tracked you down."

"Who is this?"

"Rob Murphy from the Boston Post Newspaper, I was wondering if you had any comments before we ran a story."

"What story?"

"Some kids found two 8x57 millimeter Mauser brass shells on the Vineyard yesterday. The brass was corroded, but they are Mauser shells, alright."

Sam wasn't sure he had heard right. Could you repeat that, Mr. Murphy?"

"I said that some kids went swimming yesterday and found two shell casings on South Beach about two hundred feet from where that Auxiliary Beach Patrolman was killed four years ago. The brass cartridges were matched to Manny Amaral's Mauser. You were right all along. The man they executed, Henry Miller didn't kill Joe deSilva. Manny Amaral killed him. We are running a front page story tomorrow. Would you like to comment for the newspaper?

"Have they arrested Manny Amaral?"

"Don't you know? Amaral died two years ago."

"Do you know if the Commonwealth is going to issue a public apology and a posthumous pardon to Mr. Miller?"

"I just got off the phone with the governor's office. Governor McCormack was the prosecutor on the case when he was Attorney General and is sure the jury made the right decision."

Chapter Five

The Case of the Bridge

Before Judge Sam Mathews died, he made Jake promise to do his best to clear Mr. Miller's name. Jake tried to keep his word, but the courts refused to hear an appeal, the Governor's Pardon Board turned a deaf ear and, over the passing years, three different governors returned his petitions stamped, "Denied." Still, he persevered. Jake had one last chance with the Speaker of the House of Representatives, a politician who swapped favors faster than the Red Sox traded losing pitchers. House Speaker Mace Norris actually held the power on Beacon Hill.

The ferry eased its way into the deep waters of Vineyard Sound leaving in its wake Jake's pleas and petitions to Speaker Mace Norris. He sat on a wooden deck chair in the night air, his back to the wheelhouse, sheltering him from the wind while he watched the distant lights of the mainland glow like burning embers. After a while, they dimmed and left Jake sitting under a gibbous moon listening only to the wind and sea.

Summer had turned to fall and his two sons had returned to Los Angeles. He missed them terribly. He smiled as he thought about his sons; the day in court Michael warned Steve Dichentis about having his ass kicked; the memory of watching Little Jake go starry-eyed with each stolen glance at Melanie Hayes. Like the hand of a compass pointing north, Jake felt the magic of the island drawing him home. He never thought the Vineyard was connected to the real world; it was his sanctuary and, over their summer, his boys replenished their ties to the little island.

A bulkhead door opened, and behind an arc of light, a shadowy figure stood in the doorway. A tall, thin man wearing an ice-blue windbreaker walked on deck, stopped in front of Jake and asked in a friendly voice, "Mind if I join you?"

Jake looked up. It was Walt Robinson, one of Edgartown's finest. Jake had tussled with him when Walt was a prosecuting police officer in the District Court and they grew to become friendly adversaries. "Sure Walt, take a load off 'n join me." Jake slid over another chair. "Aren't you supposed to be fighting crime on the island or something?"

Walt didn't answer. "Never mind me, how did you make out with Ernie Cumondun's case in the Dedham courthouse? The whole island is talkin' about it."

"Judge took it under advisement. We should have something in a month or so. Anything new happening on the Vineyard while I was away last week?"

Walt Robinson sat down and lazily stretched out his long legs. "Not much. Just finishing a job. Joe Barnes and me took back an escaped prisoner this morning. The two of them rowed over from Falmouth. Can you imagine? They broke out of a court holding cell on Cape Cod, stole a rowboat and then rowed seven miles across the Sound, all the way over to the island."

"Why would they do that? I mean, it's an island."

"Not the brightest bulbs is my guess. My guy said they thought they were rowing down the coast of the mainland."

"How did you catch the two?"

"We didn't. We only captured one of them."

"And the other guy?"

"When they got to the island, they ditched the rowboat, stole a car and kept riding around the island looking for Interstate Route 95. When they realized they were driving around in circles, one of them jumped out. The guy we caught eventually ran out of gas and started walking around the island in an orange prison jump-suit. That's when we nabbed him."

"What about the other one?"

"He busted into the sheriff's house at the county jail and ran off with the sheriff's wife. They are both still at large."

*

Chief Robert Paul helped Jake load his suitcase and two heavy litigation briefcases onto the back of Jake's old pickup and then got behind the wheel. When they were both comfortably seated, the big Indian turned to Jake and asked, "Did you eat dinner, boss?"

"No, not yet. We finished the case late and I beat the hell out of an Avis car to catch the eight o'clock boat to Woods Hole. Any leftovers at home?"

"I thought you would have a meal after your court business, so I did not prepare anything. I could heat the rest of the squirrel I shot and cooked. I will put it in the microwave."

"You shot a squirrel? Cooked it in the microwave?"

"It was very tasty," the Chief smacked his lips. "The hunting and eating of squirrels is a tradition our ancestors passed down. And the meat is sweet. You will not be disappointed."

"Do you eat the tail?"

"Mmmm," the Chief replied as was his practice when he did not want to answer Jake.

"How do you usually cook a squirrel?"

"I grill it on a stick outside with charcoal or I smoke it for two days with hickory chips. But this time, I was tired of eating squirrel the same way, so I made the recipe from a book on the kitchen shelf called, *The Joy of Cooking.*

"You used my ex-wife's old cookbook to cook a squirrel. What did it taste like?"

"It tasted the same to me, this joy of being cooked by a recipe."

"Like what?"

"Chicken."

"I think I'll pass on microwave squirrel. Doesn't appeal to me. Anything else at home?"

"I still have some of the goat stew I brought from my lodge and cooked for myself tonight."

"Goat stew, really?"

"I put chunks of boiled goat with my chopped special mushrooms, onions, carrots, celery stocks, vegetables, garlic and seasoning in a pot and let it cook in a creamy sauce. It is very good, Jake."

"And what does goat stew taste like?"

"Chicken."

Jake just nodded. "Maybe we should stop at Frank's place."

"If you don't want goat stew, my fish net has trapped a nice salt water eel. How would you like to eat a grilled eel, boss?"

Jake felt his stomach drop to his shoes. "Don't bother making anything special. Frank's Café is still open."

The Chief nodded, pulled out of the terminal and drove the pickup two blocks into the lot behind Frank's Island Café and Donut Shop. They pulled into a parking space and watched Frank Falcone carrying a forty-pound bag of sugar from his storage shed behind the café.

Jake opened the truck door and stood on the running board. "You must have a hell of a pile of sugar, Frank. You've been hauling it over to the restaurant for a year."

Frank smiled and set the bag down. "Well, look who's here. Bless my soul Father, if it isn't the Johnnie-Cochran-of-the-Vineyard. I told you the price of sugar was going through the roof. Now it's sky high. I stashed enough for another year. How about some help with the bags?"

Robert Paul scooped up the bag in one arm and carried it like a football into the donut shop.

"Is this a social call or a chow call?" Frank asked.

"The Chief's had supper, but I haven't eaten anything since breakfast."

"We closed ten minutes ago."

"C'mon Frank, I'm starving and the Chief wants to give me a boiled eel."

"OK, but nothing on the grille. It's closed down. All's I got left is cold chicken."

*

When Jake walked into his suite of law offices above the Grapes of Wrath bookstore the next morning, he found Penny Pacheco typing in a cubicle just outside of his private office. She recognized the shuffle of his footsteps on the stairs and did not lose a stroke on the keyboard.

"Good morning, boss. How did Ernie's case go?"

Jake put his trial bags down. "Judge in Dedham is holding the case under advisement. Could go either way."

"You're being modest, boss."

"Look, when you have chance, please sort out the two trial bags and file the material with Ernie's other stuff." Jake walked into his office and picked up a week's worth of messages. There were a half dozen requests for interviews about Ernie's case, a call from Ernie's son, a stack of messages from Ernie's wife, a call from Frank Falcone and five calls from someone named, "Jeanie." Jake thought the only one he didn't hear from in Ernie's family was Ernie Cumondun himself. But of course, he wouldn't hear anything from Ernie because Ernie was dead.

He looked at the Native New Yorker's cell number on the call back note. "What did Frank want? I saw him last night." Jake yelled through his open office door.

Penny stood in Jake's office doorway. "He called first thing. He wants to see you this morning. Says it's urgent."

Jake was going through a week's mail and kept shouting. "It's always urgent and who is this Jeanie that keeps calling? Why didn't you write down her number?"

"I am standing right here so there's no need to shout. It's Jeanie McClennon. She won't leave her number. Says you'll know what it's about."

"I don't have the foggiest."

"She's Sheriff John Francis McClennon's new wife."

Jake looked up. "Right, I heard something about her," Jake reminded himself and then remembered. "That young lady is in serious trouble. Aiding and abetting an escapee is a felony in the Commonwealth, to say nothing about what J.F. is going to do to her."

"I told her you would be in the office this morning. She said she wants to meet you right away."

"Alright, let's hear what she has to say when she comes in."

"She can't come into the office."

"Is she being held hostage?"

"She's hiding."

"It's an island for Christ sake. Where the hell can she hide on an island?"

"Are you kidding, Jake? There are a million places to hide on the Vineyard and Jeanie's family has lived here all their lives. I bet she knows them all."

The phone rang.

"I'll get it," Jake said and picked up the phone. "Law office of Jake Dellahunt, Jake Dellahunt, speaking."

"It's Frank Falcone. I need to see you this morning," Frank said tensely.

Jake motioned Penny to return to her typing and closed his office door. "Can't it wait, Frank? I've been away on Ernie Cumondun's case and have a stack of mail up to the ceiling."

"It's urgent."

"What kind of jam did you get yourself into this time?"

"You know all that sugar I have in the shed."

"Yeah."

"Well, it's hot."

Jake said nothing.

"You still there, Jake?"

"I'm listening."

"Look, I didn't know it was stolen. Two guys walked into the shop and told me it was distressed goods. They never told me they hijacked a reefer. They sold me the whole reefer."

"A reefer?"

"Yeah, they sold me a Fruehauf trailer full of sugar. Twenty thousand pounds of sugar for two grand. I got the trailer stashed off-island."

"Don't tell me. Please."

"OK. But that's not the problem."

"That's not! What's the problem then?"

"The *figli de puttanas* who sold me the sugar came in first thing this morning. They want fifty large now. If I don't come up with the money, they're going to the cops and rat me out for receiving stolen goods."

Jake shook his head. "If they turned you in, then they would be admitting they hijacked the sugar and sold it to you. Bingo, they do not collect for passing 'go,' but go straight to jail."

"They don't care, Jake. They're out on bail for a bigger beef and if they give me up, they'll walk on it."

"They're probably going to take your fifty grand and then give you up. Either way you lose."

"I was thinking of makin' them a pair of cement shoes."

"Frank, the way things are going, you'd be the first one they would collar."

"I know, but what can I do, Jake?"

"You know these two guys?"

"Sure, they're friends of a *gumba* of mine in the North End."

"Some friends you've got. I may be able to help. Just let me have their names and where I can find them. I'll see what I can do."

"They want the dough right away."

"Stall them. Tell them you're raising the money. I'll get back to you as soon as I hear anything."

"How much is this going to cost me?"

Jake thought a moment, then in an ersatz Don Corleone voice, he replied, "Someday Francis, and that day may never come, I will call upon you to do a service for me. But until that day, consider this justice a gift from me on my daughter's wedding day." Then, Jake the Godfather hung up.

*

The Cape Poge lighthouse on Chappaquiddick Island has few visitors. Jake was alone when he caught the "On Time," a barge that ferried three cars at a time across the narrows between the Vineyard and Chappaquiddick Island. He maneuvered his old Ford 4x4 off the small commuter onto Chappy and drove until he reached the deserted eastern end of the island. He turned north onto Lighthouse Road while looking back all the while at two miles of empty beaches, making sure nobody was tailing him.

He pulled in front of a white, wooden lighthouse with a black light tower rising into the blue sky. He looked around and didn't see a soul in sight. He walked up the sandy path toward the century-old lighthouse and hesitated in front of the paneled door with a brass, deadbolt nickel door lock just above a polished brass door knob.

"It's not locked, Mr. Dellahunt." It was a woman's voice from above.

Jake saw a pretty woman, wearing sun glasses, dressed in blue jeans seated with her legs dangling over a balcony about forty feet above him.

"We're up here," she said, her dark hair blowing in the breeze out of a Jackie Kennedy kerchief.

Jake didn't see anyone else, but the idea of hanging out on a lighthouse balcony with an escaped felon and his girlfriend didn't fit his job description. "No, I have a couple of bad knees and can't climb stairs. Unless you have an elevator, I'll just wait for you to come down."

Jake heard hushed pieces of momentary whispering, "We'll be right down. Just go inside and wait for us."

Jake turned the doorknob and entered. He was surprised to see a deceptively spacious open room with sunlight pouring in through a large window above a sitting area. A circular wood staircase with a carved wooden railing climbed around the walls to the top of the lighthouse. He took a seat at a table on the far end of the room and waited.

Jake heard their steps before he saw them. They came down the stairs together and walked into the sitting area holding hands. Jeanie McClennon could have been the sheriff's daughter instead of his wife. With delicately small features, she looked like a freckle-faced teenager all grown up. Jake guessed she was about half J. F.'s age. She said nothing, but sat across the table where Jake had planted himself and nervously played with her kerchief and sunglasses.

The escaped felon stood behind her, looking to be even younger than she did, small boned, and thin enough to have squeezed between a pair of jailhouse bars to make an escape. His face was bruised and swollen, his eyes half closed and chin cut up. Dressed in one of the sheriff's circus tent size t-shirts that fell to his knees, pants rolled up at the cuff and large enough at the waist to go around him twice, he looked like an abused five year-old parading around in his father's clothing.

Jake broke the ice. "How old are you, kid?"

"Old enough," the boy spit the words out and Jake saw his two front teeth had been broken.

Jake stood up and looked at the boy. "What happened to you?"

"What's it to you?" the kid snarled.

195

"Look, I came out here to help you. So chill with the attitude."

"If you came to help me, give me a gun."

"Why would you need a gun?"

"To shoot the son-of-a-bitches who did this to me. And worse."

"What were they holding you on over in Falmouth before you broke out?"

"What do you give a shit?"

Jeanie McClennon shouted at the boy, "Stop it. Mr. Dellahunt came here to help you." She turned to Jake, "He was charged with possession of marijuana with intent to sell."

"How much was he holding?"

The kid answered quickly, "It was a bull shit charge. A couple of ounces."

Jake was losing patience. "They don't charge anyone with intent to sell for holding a couple of ounces. Why did you call me, Mrs. McClennon?"

A figure walked into the lighthouse. "I asked her to call you," boomed a familiar voice from the doorway.

Jake turned around to see Sheriff J. F. McClennon standing at the entrance. He wondered how he could have been followed – unless McClennon did not follow him, unless McClennon was already there. "What the hell is going on?"

Jeanie McClennon walked over to her husband and kissed him. He put his arm around her waist and they stepped over to Jake. "I asked Jeannie to call you," the sheriff repeated.

*

Chief Robert Paul pulled the roast chicken and apple dumplings out of the oven and brought them over to the table where Jake was sitting. He placed the food on a large serving plate next to a bowl of salad and baked potatoes and then sat down. "There was some guy looking for you today, boss."

"Was it one of those fuckers from the IRS?"

"No, it was Ernie Cumondun's son. I do not understand this business you are doing for Mr. Cumondun," the big Indian said as he cut up the chicken on the platter and then spilled most of it in his plate. "Ernie is dead, so who will pay you for your work? That is why you never have money, Jake Dellahunt. You take cases of dead people who cannot pay you."

"Oh, I'll get paid, alright. Do we have anything to drink?"

The Wampanoag rose and pulled two bottles of beer out of the fridge. "You will be paid only if the Great Spirit breathes life into the dead body of Ernie Cumondun," he said and set one bottle down in front of Jake and took a swig out of the other. "Your two sons called from California today."

"Did you talk to them? How are they?"

"Little Jake wants to know if you have a case he can work on since you made him your junior partner and Michael says they are planning to come to the island over their Christmas break."

"Over Christmas vacation, you say. Let's pencil that on the kitchen calendar. I'll call them back right after we finish eating."

The huge Wampanoag stopped eating and drained the bottle of beer dry in a couple of gulps. "Maybe Maggie will come, too. It will be like old times."

"Don't get your hopes up," Jake replied. "She's still got it in for me."

"Do you like the chicken, boss? I raised it from a chick in my lodge in Gay Head."

"Was this your pet chicken?"

"I think it is better to eat a chicken you know than one you do not know," the Indian replied and helped himself to the rest of the dark meat. "I do not understand this Ernie business. How can Ernie Cumondun pay you now if he is dead?"

"His trust will pay."

"I, too, would like to have this trust thing pay all my bills. Can you make this trust for me?"

"You have to put something into the trust before it will pay your bills."

"I have many things I could put into this trust. All of my lobster traps and my fishing nets."

"I think you need something more valuable."

"What could be more valuable than traps to catch food to keep yourself alive?"

"Good point, but the trust probably couldn't pay your bills with flounders and lobsters."

"Then tell me how did Ernie Cumondun make a trust?"

"Ernie probably was the richest guy on the island. He bought a thousand acres of land on the island in West Tisbury and, along with the property, he received a 1785 deed that conveyed an irrevocable legal franchise and exclusive non-cancelable right from the Commonwealth to erect a private structure over all abutting navigable waterways."

"I do not understand these trick lawyer words."

"It means Ernie has the right to build a bridge from the shores of Martha's Vineyard to the mainland."

Robert Paul stopped eating and gasped, "How can that be possible?"

"It's structurally and legally possible. They have built bridges in the United States that are longer in places like, Lake Pontchartrain in New Orleans, the Bay Bridge to Oakland and the bridges over the Florida Keys."

"But the government would never let anyone build a bridge to the mainland. That is not possible."

"I don't know about that. After the Revolutionary War, the states were broke. They paid for a good part of the war and wound up heavily in debt. So many states, including Massachusetts, raised money by selling irrevocable rights and privileges to construct private bridges and toll roads. When Ernie Cumondun bought that huge amount of land on the island, the rights to erect a bridge ran with deeded property and he wound up owning in perpetuity the right to build a bridge to the mainland. It's the same kind of charter the Commonwealth gave to the steamship authority to run ferry boats and charge passengers. "

"You must not let them do this thing, Jake. It will ruin everything."

"Ernie put the land and bridge rights into a trust and made Judge Sam the Trustee. When Sam Mathews died, I became the successor trustee. The trust went effective the moment Ernie Cumondun died."

"So building a bridge to America is up to you?"

"Yes and no. Currently, I'm the trustee and have the right to do whatever I think is best, but there are many rich and powerful people who would pay tens of millions for the land and the rights to build a toll bridge. Of course, Ernie's wife and his son and others in his family will only receive money if I sell the property. So, they petitioned the court to have me removed as trustee."

"What will you do?"

"For the moment, nothing. It's in the hands of a judge over at the Dedham Probate Court. I can't do anything until the court either confirms or replaces me as the sole trustee."

Chief Robert Paul sat for a while saying nothing. He stood up and began clearing the dishes from the table while Jake went into the living room to call his sons in California. He sat on the couch talking to Michael first and then to Little Jake.

"Mom says she's thinking about coming with us to the Vineyard over Christmas vacation. Do you think that would be alright, Dad?" Jake's oldest son asked over the phone.

"I can't think of anything better. Tell her we'll fix up the back deck for an extra bedroom. We can start working on it right away."

"I'll tell her, Dad. Do you have cases for me while we're on-island?"

"Tell Mother Ernie Cumondun died last month and I am the sole trustee for his property and bridge rights. I am going to have to deal with the islanders about building a bridge over to the mainland."

"Dad, you can't be real. You can't be thinking about building a bridge. That's so uncool."

"I wish it were just that simple. The whole island is being torn apart by rich summer people and others who come here for a peaceful get-away. Then there are the rest of us, who have to make an all-year-round living in three months. We pay top dollar for everything shipped here by ferry from a bottle of milk to a pair of diapers twelve months a year. A bridge would make the island more affordable for everyone."

"It would spoil the island. A bridge would kill the place. Dad, don't do it."

Jake heard the concern in his son's voice. "Look, the matter is in the court's hands, so for the moment, let's not worry about it."

"If it's left to you, what are you going to do?"

"I really don't know."

*

It was an Indian summer island day and Jake walked back slowly in the warm October sun from the post office towards the Grapes of Wrath Bookstore on Main Street. He glanced at the mail and saw a letter from the Norfolk Probate Court in Dedham. It seemed much too soon to receive a decision about Ernie's case. He stopped a moment and opened the envelope. It was a Court Order. He looked at the last few lines. "Therefore, before Judgment shall be rendered, This Court hereby allows the Massachusetts Legislature a period of ten days from the date hereof to file an Amicus Curiae Brief, a written argument in support of removing Jacoby Dellahunt, Esq., as sole trustee of the Ernie Cumondun Trust."

Jake read the entire order, shook his head and returned the piece of paper to the envelope. Jake guessed somebody on the Hill smelled money and a private toll bridge reeked of it. The state legislature stood squarely with the Cumondun family to unseat him as trustee, sell the land and build a bridge over to the mainland –

something he thought for the very first time might not be a good idea.

As he walked down Main Street with the mail in hand, he saw flashing red lights on top of a pair of parked state police cruisers drawing a crowd of onlookers. Two state troopers dressed in blue uniforms wearing spit and polished, black leather belts and high boots stood on either side of the outside stairs leading to his office on the second floor. Jake stopped in front of them.

"I'm Attorney Jake Dellahunt. What's this all about?"

"Please step into the unmarked car behind you, sir. The detective wants to talk to you."

Jake said nothing. He followed the troopers to a white Ford Interceptor and slipped into the front seat beside a man dressed in a blue suit with a narrow, red, 50's flea market tie dangling from the unbuttoned collar of his wash 'n wear special. It was James Doyle, the island's only state police detective. He was a short, beefy, square-face, hard drinking cop. Jake knew him from court and always kept his distance. The word in courthouse lobby was Doyle hated lawyers and in that, he wasn't alone.

Jake put on his game face. "Pretty good show you're putting on, Detective Doyle. What can I do for you?"

"Let's keep this little talk of ours private," Doyle said. He leaned over and shut the passenger door. "You met with an escaped prisoner, yesterday. Why didn't you tell us?"

"If I did speak to him, and mind you I'm not admitting it, I'm under no obligation to tell you, Doyle."

Doyle faced Jake. "Cut the lawyer crap, Dellahunt. I could charge you with aiding and abetting and obstruction of justice right now."

"For what?"

"Where's the kid?"

"You're the detective."

Doyle opened his jacket and pulled out a cigarette. "I know he's on the run and dangerous."

"Do you really think he's dangerous? Top of the Most Wanted List? I heard the only thing he was carrying was a Stop 'n Shop bag of weed. Some pervert in Barnstable used his face for a punching bag and his ass for pleasure, so first chance he takes off for a vacation on the Vineyard."

"Look, I am going to cuff you if you don't tell me where I can find him."

"What if I told you he was over at the *Gazette* having his bashed-in face and beaten-up body photographed for their lead story about prison brutality? We could stick your picture right next to his for threatening to jail his lawyer."

Doyle lit his cigarette and blew the smoke at Jake. "So you admit to being his lawyer."

"Just being a lawyer doesn't warrant grounds for arrest. Otherwise you'd be out arresting every lawyer on the island."

Doyle smiled. "Not a bad idea, counselor."

Doyle might have been a bigger shit than two tons of smoking manure, but Jake knew he didn't make detective for being stupid. "And what if I told you he might be willing to surrender under certain conditions?"

The detective thought a moment and stretched back in his seat. "Alright Dellahunt, we'll play it your way for a while. You want to trade. Tell me, what do you want in exchange for the kid?"

"The kid is not going back to Barnstable, Doyle. They'll kill him over there or he'll hang himself for sure if he goes back. I'll plead him out in Edgartown and he stays on the island. He does his time in the island jailhouse."

"You mean the country club in Edgartown?"

"At least he'll be safe in the island lockup."

"What makes you think I can deal?"

"If you can't, you might wanna talk to the D.A. over in Barnstable. Your escaped prisoner is an islander, born and bred right here. The Vineyard is small, but there are a couple of thousand other islanders who will hide this kid when they find out what happened to him in the Barnstable Detention Center."

"Nobody gives a crap what happens on this lousy island."

"Don't be thinking his story is going to stay put on this island. We got half the people on *60 Minutes*, owners, editors and reporters from the *New York Times* to the *Washington Post* living here."

Doyle straightened up. "You'll plead your client to both the drug and the escape charges?"

"No more than eighteen months, both sentences running concurrently."

"And you'll keep this out of the newspapers?"

"Not forever."

"I'll talk to the Barnstable D. A."

"You have him draw up a sentencing agreement and both of you put it in writing, signed in triplicate."

"Don't you trust me, Jake?"

"Good agreements make good friends and, by the way Doyle, only my friends call me, Jake."

Jake left Detective Doyle smoking his cigarette behind the wheel and took the stairs to his office. As soon as he opened the door, Penny Pacheco jumped up. "What did the cops want with you?"

"Why didn't you call my cell and tell me James Doyle was about to bushwhack me with second hand smoke?"

"Sorry."

"Did I get any calls?"

"You got a call from State Speaker Mace Norris and Frank called and wants to know what you're doing about whatever he says you're supposed to be doing."

"The Speaker of the House of Representatives, you say. What did he want?"

"He wants to see you for lunch at Locke-Ober's, if you come into Boston Monday."

"Did he say what it was about?"

"No."

Jake thought a moment. "How does Monday look?"

"It's an open day. No appointments or court appearances. Instead of hanging around with the little people watching the nails rust, you could be hobnobbing with the rich and famous at Locke-Ober's, boss."

"OK, maybe you're right. I'll go to the lunch meeting, but don't forget the admonition in the Bible about hobnobbing with the rich and famous."

"What's the Bible say?"

"That the tallest blade of grass is always the first to be cut down."

*

Jake's cabin fever turned into culture shock as he snaked through the traffic on the Southeast Expressway and drove through the canyons of Boston high-rises. He parked his car in a Government Center garage for a day's pay on the island and walked down Washington Street into the crowded restaurant.

Locke-Ober's Restaurant is a hidden treasure, buried in a downtown Boston alley for a couple of centuries. It's a dark mahogany place where the old-money white crowd meets for lunch. It's the place where Enrico Caruso cooked his own sweetbreads; where John F. Kennedy ordered lobster stew, drank the broth and gave the meat to the waiter; where a dying man came for his last lunch; and where, when regular customers pass away, their plates are turned over and their chairs are leaned up against the table. It's the place where women were long excluded and lawyers and politicians tell one another stories no one believes.

Speaker Mace Norris was a large man, who did not go unnoticed. Few in the restaurant failed to greet him before they took their seats although he didn't take his regular table, but sat in the far corner of the first floor café. The lunch crowd had quickly filled the restaurant with congenial conversation, and venerable waiters from a European world long past, dressed in traditional black uniforms with long white bistro aprons, hustled around the room. Jake walked through the small vestibule and the *maître d'* immediately sat him across the table from the Speaker.

"I took the liberty of ordering you a martini, but I cancelled it. Someone told me you don't drink anymore."

Jake did not respond.

"Of course, if you would like a drink…"

"Just an iced tea. Look, Mr. Norris…"

"Call me Mace."

"Look Mace, this is awkward. I don't know if it's appropriate to be having lunch when I am the sole trustee of Ernie Cumondun's trust and you're in court trying to replace me."

The Speaker leaned his elbows on the table. "There's nothing wrong with the two of us having lunch in a public place and, if you feel uncomfortable, we won't talk about the case."

"Alright, but I don't want even the appearance of impropriety. I'll pay for my own meal."

"Fine with me," Mace Norris handed a menu to Jake.

Jake almost choked when he looked at the prices. He immediately regretted telling Norris he was going Dutch, but it was too late. Norris signaled the waiter to come over. When the waiter did not come right away, Norris bent over and whispered, "These waiters are all guineas and they're richer than their Jew customers."

Jake felt a burning in his gut.

The waiter approached and Norris sat up and said in a loud voice. "Try their fish. It's the best."

"Yes, sir, Mr. Norris. The fish is fresh today."

"Jake, this is Tommy. He's worked here - how long have you been here, Tommy?"

"This is my-a fortieth year," the waiter replied with a noticeable Italian accent.

"This is Mr. Dellahunt, Tommy. He's a famous lawyer on Martha's Vineyard."

"I know Mr. Dellahunt."

Norris was amazed. "You do?"

"My family has-a nice-a house across from the Tabernacle in Oak Bluffs," the waiter replied. "You ran-a property title for us a few years ago. We are the DeScuzio family."

Norris winked at Jake and began to order. "I'll start with half dozen East Coast Oysters, Tommy and give my friend here a dozen Little Neck Clams. Would you like some of their JFK Lobster Stew, Jake?"

"No thanks."

"Well, just bring us a small cup. You have to taste this, Jake. You'll love it," the big man said.

"How about their Saracena Olive Salad?"

"No," Jake replied.

"Tommy, give him a small Locke Ober's house salad and I'll have the Dover Sole."

The waiter asked, "What-a will you have Mr. Dellahunt?"

"I'll have the small *filet mignon*."

"How would you like it cooked?"

"*Medi rari, per favore*," Jake responded.

"*Lei parla italiano?*" the waiter asked.

"*Lo parlo, basta.*"

"The sauce-a we have, *le salse oggi sono Bordelaise, Marrow, Béarnaise, Roquefort, Locke' aglio del Yuzu-Aioli, Limone della Blanc, Soia del Cappero, Buerre della Bistecca*, for the potato, we have-a *Mashed, Pommes Frites, Gratin Dauphinois, I pancake di patata, crema acida, Apple Compote, Baked, latteria di Idaho, Vermont, punte affumicate della pancetta affumicata per i* for vegetables, we have *legumbres che abbiamo cotto l'asparago Hollandaise alla griglia, il broccolo scremato di SpinachSteamed, il broccolo bianco di Fondue Chinese del formaggio cheddar, lo zenzero, GarlicHand hanno selezionato il pisello ShootsHaricot*

Verts i mushrooms, *funghi arrostiti, degli anelli di cipolla di ShallotsCrispy della selezione,"* the waiter said and waited while Jake decided.

"Quale, Signore Dellahunt?"

"Scegliete, Tommy. You choose."

The waiter walked away without writing a word and Mace Norris, with mouth agape, suspiciously asked, "You speak Italian?"

"Yeah, my father was Irish, but my mom was a real genuine guineau."

Neither of them spoke for a few minutes. The waiter returned from the raw bar with the littlenecks and oysters, set the salads on the table and quickly walked away.

Jake threw down a couple of littlenecks and they seemed to cool him down. "Why did you really want to meet me?"

"I wanted to buy some insurance."

"You think I'm an insurance salesman?"

Norris raised both hands in the air. "Of course, not. Ever go to Las Vegas and play blackjack? You can make a side bet when the dealer shows an Ace up, that he also has 10 in the hole, giving him 21. It's called, 'insurance.'"

"So you think I'm holding an unbeatable hand and you want to make a side bet?"

"No, not at all. I'm told the decision to remove you could go either way. But just in case we can't unseat you as trustee in a courtroom, I'm here to ask you what it would take…"

Jake finished the sentence. "To walk away and leave Ernie's family in control of the trust?"

Norris continued. "Like I say, I'm here to buy insurance. But before I shop for insurance, let me ask you a question. Why did you agree to meet me if you weren't looking for something?"

"I made a promise to my partner long ago to vindicate one of his clients. The state threw the switch on an innocent guy. I was hoping to convince you to help me keep my promise."

"Is that all you want?"

"Mace, this is not some political trade-off."

"Wake up, Jake. Everything is political. We're talking about things you need; something only someone on Beacon Hill can do for you, like a full pardon for Henry Miller, a suspended sentence for that island kid you represent instead of being sent back to prison in Barnstable where he's not going to last a month."

Norris had done his homework, but Jake did not reply.

"And I hear there's an opening for a second judgeship in the Edgartown District Court that needs to be filled. The governor owes me big time."

Jake continued eating his salad. A few minutes elapsed without a word.

"Alright then, it always comes down to money. How much do you need?" Norris asked brazenly. "Don't you understand what's going on? I've got real estate developers and land speculators calling night and day. International hotel chains want to build a thousand rooms and put in casinos. Resort lines and travel companies are salivating to get their hands on the bridge rights and the property. This is a multi-billion dollar deal. The island could be bigger than Las Vegas. It will be the greatest tourist attraction on the east coast. At twenty bucks a pop, we figure more than a quarter of a million cars will go over the new Vineyard bridge every year."

Jake felt his heart almost stop. He looked up. "The state will never let it happen."

"It's a done deal up at the state house. You're the last piece in the puzzle. Just give me a number and it's yours. Whatever you need."

Jake put down his fork down and stopped eating. "Are you serious?"

Norris smiled deliciously at Jake's naivety. "Serious as a trunk full of cash," the Speaker said and leaned over the table. "If you need proof of my sincerity, just surrender that kid you're hiding on the island to Doyle. Lieutenant Doyle's gonna put him back on the street with a suspended."

"Wait a minute. I thought Doyle was only a State Police Detective."

"We promoted him to lieutenant today for helping your kid out of a jam."

*

"How did your meeting go with Speaker Norris, yesterday?" Penny asked as Jake settled into his early morning office routine.

"Great! He wants to turn the island into the Las Vegas strip."

"Jake, you're so funny."

"We'll see how funny I am. Call the sheriff and tell him to have that escaped prisoner over at the courthouse in Edgartown at 2:00 p.m. sharp."

"You want me to call Sheriff McClennon? I thought the prisoner took off with Mrs. McClennon."

"He did. The escaped prisoner is her kid brother."

"What?"

"Hello. He's Sheriff John Francis McClennon's new brother-in-law."

"Oh my God!"

"Then call Doyle at the state police barracks in Oak Bluffs and the Barnstable County District Attorney. Tell them I'm surrendering their escaped prisoner to the District Court in Edgartown."

The phone rang and Penny picked it up. After a moment of conversation she whispered, "It's someone with an accent."

"That narrows it down. Get his name."

"Tommy DeScuzio. He says he was your waiter at Locke Ober's Restaurant." She handed the phone to Jake. "You probably left your credit card there." She laughed and then walked out of his office to call the sheriff, Doyle and the D.A."

Jake took the telephone. "Tommy, how are you?"

"I'm-a good. *Bene, grazie.* But I'm-a little worried about you, Mr. Dellahunt."

"Me?"

"Sure. You help-a my family with the house on the island and so now I can help you."

"I was happy to lend a hand. Hey, we're *Italiani.*"

"You know-a that Norris big shot you were with yesterday at the restaurant. He is a racist. He never tip me. He don't tip anyone here. He-a thinks he owns the place. Well, he don't, but that's another story. After you and him left, the feds came in snooping around and ask me what you and him say. I wanted you to know. You should-a keep away from that man."

"Who was asking questions about our conversation?"

"I don't-a know their name, but the *maître d'* tell me they are from the U. S. Attorney's office. He tell-a me to answer their questions, but I don't-a say nothing. Please be careful, Mr. Dellahunt. Some-a-thing bad is going to happen."

*

Judge J. J. McNaught, a short man, with a sober look about him, took his seat on the bench at the stroke of two o'clock. Jake's client, his face still bruised and battered, once again dressed in his orange prison jump suit, sat between Jake and Sheriff McClennon at the defense table. Across from them, the newly promoted state police Lieutenant James Doyle sat with Al Norton, the Duke's County District Attorney and Phil Lawson, an Assistant D. A. representing the Barnstable County District Attorney's office.

Judge McNaught read the papers on the bench and looked up. "These are serious charges Mr. Dellahunt. Your client is charged with possession of a Class D substance with intent to sell and a charge of escape. Jurisdiction lies in Barnstable County on both complaints. These charges should be heard by a judge on the mainland. What do you have to say?"

"If it pleases the court, we are surrendering the prisoner voluntarily and ask this court to accept jurisdiction for arraignment and to accept a plea at this time. My client is an islander and you can plainly see how he was treated in the Barnstable County Jail. He has returned to this county to accept the judgment of the court and we ask only he not be returned to the mainland."

"Is that acceptable to the District Attorney in Barnstable County, Mr. Lawson?"

"Yes and without objection."

"And Al?"

"It's acceptable to this county, also."

"Alright then, Dukes County will accept the case. How does your client want to plea?"

Jake was still standing. "Guilty on both charges."

"I will enter your client's guilty plea and we can have a sentencing hearing in 30 days for sentence recommendations."

Doyle stood up and interrupted the judge. "Excuse me Your Honor. May I speak? I am the arresting officer and the police prosecutor in this case. The defendant is nineteen years old with no priors and was abused in jail. The government is not seeking any further jail time and recommends a two year suspended sentence on both charges to run concurrently."

"Do you concur, Mr. Dellahunt?"

Jake nodded affirmatively and the judge banged down his gavel and said, "So ordered. Two years on each charge, sentences to run concurrently. Sentences are hereby suspended. You are free to leave young man."

Jake walked out of the courtroom wondering why he had ever bothered to go to law school.

*

When Jake Dellahunt returned to his law office that afternoon, he found Ernie Cumondun's widow, Mitzi Cumondun and her son, Arnost, sitting in the waiting room. Mitzi was one of those frazzled, old bleached blonds you see in Florida with a face pulled as tight as Saran wrap from one too many lifts. Ernie once told Jake he spent two hundred thousand one year having Mitzi's tummy tucked in, her fat sucked out, her breasts lifted, her ass lowered, her face firmed, her hair thickened and her vagina tightened. Mitzi and Arnost were a pair. She rarely traveled anywhere on the island without her fifty-two year-old son, Arnost Cumondun or "Arnie," as she called him, whom Jake always thought was badly in need of a brain transplant.

"Mitzi, what the hell are you two doing here?"

"We come to talk to you, Jake."

"To talk to you," Arnost repeated.

"I asked them to leave, but they just keep sitting there," Penny added.

Jake shook his head. "You know I can't talk to you. You're in litigation to replace me as trustee. The rules don't allow me to talk to you without your lawyers present."

"I fired my lawyers this morning."

"Yeah, we fired them," Arnost reiterated.

Mitzi turned to Arnost. "Arnie, shut up. I'm doing the talking to Jake."

"Okay, Mother."

"I want you to represent us, Jake."

"I always thought you were off your rocker, but this is one for the *Boston Bar Journal*. Let me get this straight. You want to hire me for your case against me. "

"Do you want me to call the cops, boss?"

"No, I want to hear why Mitzi wants to hire me for her lawyer in her case against me."

Mitzi pulled out a cigarette and Arnost lit it.

"There's no smoking in this office," Penny sternly warned.

Mitzi blew smoke at Penny and then stood up. She moved close to Jake. "You know Ernie and I have always loved you. The lawsuit is not really against you in particular. It's against the trustee of Ernie's trust."

"I am the trustee of Ernie's trust."

She took Jake's arm. "Of course you are, Jake. Take me into your office and we can discuss all of this."

"Mitzi, are you saying you are going to pay me to get rid of me?"

Mitzi's tone became seductive as a cat in heat. "Let's not talk out here. Let's go into your office and you can tell me what you really want."

"I'm not going anywhere until you tell me what this is all about."

Penny shouted. "Let me call the Sheriff. He owes you for today."

"Hang on, Penny. I want to know what this is all about."

Mitzi Cumondun pushed Jake away. "Alright, I'll tell you what I want you to do. I want you to make those nasty little men from the United States Attorney's office go away."

"So that's it. You've been talking to Mace Norris."

"What if I have?"

"He put you up to all this lawsuit business, didn't he?"

"What if he did?"

"Why do you think all those nasty little men want to talk to you?"

Mitzi said nothing.

"That's not a rhetorical question, Mitzi. Don't you know Mace Norris already sold the land and bridge rights to some Las Vegas mogul who's just drooling at the idea of bringing millions of people over from America? All he needs is a trustee to sign the deal. You sell out, turn a pretty penny and Mace Norris gets very rich for putting the deal together."

"There's nothing wrong with making money, Jake. You could make a lot of money, too."

"How? By turning every street on the island into a Los Angelean grid-locked freeway? Why do you think the feds want to talk to you? Norris is using his position as Speaker of the House to broker a sale and keep the legislature from intervening. The last couple of House Speakers went to jail for the same thing. Influence peddling is a crime and the people who make money from influence peddling are charged as co-conspirators. The feds know you're helping Norris. You're in real trouble Mitzi."

"I could tell them I never made any deal with Norris."

"They'll prosecute you for lying to a federal agent or worse."

"I could refuse to sell."

"Too late to change your mind. It's not the sale. It's the arrangement you made with Norris to sell. No, you're in too deep now to walk away."

Mitzi walked back to a chair and sat down for a moment. She looked up dejectedly. "That's why I'm here. Ernie always told me if I were ever in real trouble, hire Jake Dellahunt. Please Jake, will you help us?"

"Now that you're my client, let's go into my office and talk for a while. Maybe I have a way out for everyone."

*

The following morning Jake sat alone on the outside deck of Frank's Island Café and Donut Shop sipping his second cup of joe while he waited for an early ferry.

After a minute, Frank Falcone walked out onto the deck. "Don't you answer your phone messages, counselor? I called a half dozen times yesterday afternoon."

"I was busy all afternoon and most of last night."

"Yeah, I heard."

The island was a rumor mill and Jake wondered if anyone knew what he was planning to do. "What did you hear, Frank?"

"How you walked Sheriff McClennon's kid brother-in-law out of Judge McNaught's court."

"What exactly did you hear?" Jake asked and held his breath fearful he would hear Mace Norris' name come up.

"Nothing except you worked a deal with the cops, 'cause they bent the kid over in the shower and all."

214

Jake didn't want to talk about it. "You got customers inside Frank."

"They can wait. Let me ask you, *consulari*, how did you solve my problem?"

"What do you mean?"

"I would like to know what you did to those two guys."

"Me, nothing."

"Those two mugs showed up in my shop yesterday."

"Looking for fifty grand?"

"No. They were on their knees begging me to forgive them. They were crying, pleading for their lives on their knees. It was embarrassing; there were customers in the shop. They wanted me to forgive them. They says I held their lives in my hands. What the hell did you do?"

"I told you, I didn't do a thing. What did you do? Did you forgive them?"

"They gave me an envelope with money."

"Did you take the money?"

"They give me back my two grand and says they moved the trailer to another location."

"Well, sounds like you're out of the woods. I guess you're back to square one, Frank."

"I don't know what you did."

"Sometimes it's better you don't know."

"Come on, Jake."

Jake reluctantly responded after a moment. "It was a tricky situation you got yourself into, Frank. You couldn't go to the cops and have them taken down for extortion and I am certain the courts wouldn't help you, so I did what any good lawyer would do under the circumstances."

"That's what I'm asking. Come on Jake, tell me."

"Okay. No big deal. I went to the mob. I called in a favor from one of my old clients in Providence, Rhode Island."

"You sent the Providence mob after them?"

"Frank, it's over. Don't ask too many questions. You don't want to know. Just enjoy your peace of mind from this point in time until the next jam you get yourself into - which I'm sure is in the works as we speak."

"Jake, half that reefer is still filled with sugar. Can you get it for me? I could sure use the rest of the sugar. We could go partners in it."

Jake put the cover back on his coffee and stood up. "Frank, do you know the people in Providence who owed me a favor?"

"No, I don't know them."

"Well, if you so much as hint I go partners with you in anything illegal, they're going to come over to the Café and Donut Shop and put one large donut hole in your head. *Capisce paisano?*"

"*Si, capisco.*"

*

Jake said his good-byes to Frank and walked two short blocks carrying his coffee to the parking lot behind his office. It took him fifteen minutes to drive to Oak Bluffs, park and board the compact *Island Queen* bound for Falmouth Harbor on Cape Cod. As the early morning commuter crept out of the dock, Jake sipped some of the brew. When he realized it had turned cold, he threw out the rest of the cup. He thought about finding another place for his morning coffee, but dismissed the idea. It somehow didn't live up to the challenge of keeping Frank out of jail.

It was always a tad cheerless for Jake to leave Martha's Vineyard even though he knew he would probably be taking the next boat back within the hour or so. At a quarter past ten, the ferry eased into its berth in Falmouth. Jake spotted the black limousine at the dock and waited until the few other passengers had disembarked before stepping onto the walkway. As Jake moved close to the limousine, a back window rolled down halfway revealing a large man sitting in the back seat. There was no mistaking Mace Norris. He greeted Jake and then invited him into the limo.

Jake thought better. "Let's go for a walk."

"Alright," Norris responded, opened the door and, because of his weight, struggled to get out. He stood up and buttoned his overcoat to keep out the cold fall wind and, shoving his hands into his overcoat pockets, he joined Jake as they both walked down the wooden dock listening only to the wind and seagulls. Neither Jake nor the Speaker said a word as they moved to the far end of the dock and leaned against the railing while looking out at the water. They were alone waiting for the other to begin the conversation.

"How was the trip over?" Speaker Norris finally said.

Jake responded thoughtfully. "Fine, fine. I heard you had a house on the Cape and thought this would be a good place to meet."

"My cottage is not too far from here in Marston Mills." Norris moved close to Jake and cautiously whispered to him, "Let's get down to business. I assume you want to tell me something you didn't want to talk about on a telephone."

Jake didn't whisper back and he didn't hesitate a moment. His response was direct and the words easily came out just as he had planned the prior evening. "I'm here to tell you the U. S. Attorney is after you."

Norris scoffed at the statement. "That's hardly news, counselor. Mr. Goody Two-Shoes is always looking for a way to make my life miserable and a name for himself. Don't you know he wants to run for governor at my expense?"

Jake had considered Norris would probably dismiss the peril he faced. "There's a lot more here. It's far more serious than just a political ploy for publicity. The U. S. Attorney is focusing his investigation on your role in having the trustee sell Ernie Cumondun's land and bridge rights."

"How do you know he's after me for the bridge and land deal on the Vineyard?"

"I have it from two reliable sources."

The Speaker considered Jake's information for a moment and after he digested the warning, he said, "Is that all you have for me? Because I hope you didn't drag me down here all the way from Boston to just tell me the feds are looking into the trust deal."

Jake quickly responded, "No, there's more. Your pal, Mitzi Cumondun fired her lawyers yesterday afternoon and dismissed her law case to replace me as trustee. So now your lawyers don't have to file an Amicus brief because the case is over."

Jake saw he had struck gold. There was a noticeable change in Norris. His face turned red and he excitedly cried out, "Why would she dismiss her case?"

"I dismissed it for her. She hired me to be her lawyer."

"You're her lawyer?" he repeated in disbelief.

"How can that be? It's impossible. And tell me, why? Why would she drop her law suit and hire you?"

"The feds are threatening to subpoena her. They want to know every detail of your deal with her and what she knows about your arrangement selling the land and the bridge rights in Las Vegas to Harold Alexson."

"The U. S. Attorney knows about my deal in Las Vegas with Hal Alexson?"

"Not at this point. You told her all about the buyer you had lined up in Las Vegas, didn't you? How do you think I found out? If she tells them about Alexson and they subpoena him, you know he's going to squawk like a cat with his tail on fire. He's going to tell them what you promised legislative leaders to sit on their hands and how much you and everyone else on Beacon Hill are going to take home from the deal. He's not going to lie for you."

"Oh Lord."

"Of course, that's if they subpoena Mitzi and only if Mrs. Cumondun tells them about Harold Alexson."

"Now that you know about Hal, they can subpoena you too," Norris blurted out.

"Probably." Jake answered although he was aware he could assert client privilege and not be forced to tell anyone what Mitzi had told him.

"Oh, Jesus! Good God! What are you and Mitzi going to tell the feds if they subpoena you?" Norris cried out.

"Well Mace, that really depends on you."

*

It took a few days to complete planning the announcement. One week later, Martha's Vineyard Regional High School's gym and basketball court overflowed with people from far and wide waiting to hear the decision about building a bridge over to the mainland. Homeowners and residents quickly filled the five hundred chairs high school janitors had set out on the floor of the basketball court. Soon the stands on either side teemed with people. Those who could not find seats stood in the hallways and corridors where loud speakers and television sets had been placed on makeshift wall shelving. A dozen officials from Boston and the island sat along with Jake in metal bridge chairs on a platform next to the far wall. Newspaper reporters waited impatiently in the first row and television cameras and broadcast equipment were strewn about the floor around them.

The noise of the crowd faded quickly when the audience saw Jake rise to his feet and stand in front of the microphone. Like a contagion traveling through the audience, the hushed crowd turned silent as a stone, holding its collective breath in anticipation of the announcement. They had no idea of what to expect. It had been the only topic of conversation on the island for weeks and speculation about the bridge ran rampant. Jake looked into the mass of people shoehorned into the gymnasium and then glanced to the side of the dais to assure himself Robert Paul was standing ready to protect him from the crowd when the announcement was made.

Jake began. "Most of you knew Ernie Cumondun. He made his home on this island, but traveled to Japan, Korea and China to make his fortune. And make his fortune, he did. Almost a half century ago, he bought and placed in trust for his wife, Mitzi and his family the last treasure of the island, a thousand acres of land in West Tisbury, with its beachfront, wild rolling hills and beach grass meadows, along with the ancient bridge rights that were transferred to him with the parcel. He named my old law partner and his best friend, Judge Sam Mathews as the trustee in control of the property and the bridge rights. When Judge Sam died, I was named the successor trustee and when Ernie passed away a number of months ago, I was asked to make a decision about selling the land and the rights to erect a bridge across Vineyard Sound to the St. Elizabeth islands and westward to Woods Hole on the mainland.

"Until a week ago or so, I was uncertain what to do. Mrs. Cumondun, Mitzi, sought the advice of a number of people, several of whom are sitting on this platform. Although she is currently out of the country on a world cruise for the year, I can assure you she has been in touch with me throughout the decision-making process and she is in complete agreement with my decision.

"The person who gave her the most direction and help is sitting right here on the podium behind me. He has explored the disposition of the land and the bridge rights and has been instrumental in maximizing the future benefits for all residents. He is responsible for making the arrangement for the disposition of the bridge and property. I am pleased to introduce to you the Massachusetts Speaker of the House of Representatives, Speaker Mace Norris."

The audience applauded politely as the large man stood. Mace shook hands with Jake and, extending his right arm onto Jake's left shoulder, he moved to the microphone, holding Jake in place on the podium with one hand and the microphone in the other.

Norris smiled at the audience. "Thank you. Mr. Dellahunt. I am here to announce two public decisions today," he said. "First, would you hold the mike for a moment?" the Speaker asked while he pulled a piece of paper from his pocket and held it up to the crowd. "This is something I believe is long overdue."

Norris opened the document and read aloud. "'Almost seventy years ago, in the heat of war and in an atmosphere of prejudice that blinded justice, Judge Sam Mathews defended an innocent man whom the state wrongfully executed. Today, the state acknowledges its mistake and grants to Henry Miller, island resident and a man of principle, a full and unconditional pardon, a dismissal of charges against him and a public apology.' This document," Norris declared, "is signed by the Governor of the Commonwealth of Massachusetts."

Norris handed the document to Jake and shook his hand once again. Jake held the paper up for all to see. "I am pleased to accept this pardon on behalf Henry Miller and Judge Mathews who so desperately wanted to see his client exonerated of all charges. Thank you, Mr. Norris." The crowd applauded respectfully and waited for the next shoe to drop.

Jake waited for the audience to quiet. "We have reached the moment of decision. It has not been an easy decision. I have in my hand the deed of transfer that holds the future fate of the entire island. I now ask Roy Hearn to step forward."

A small man in an expensive double breasted gray suit stood up from the row of bridge chairs on the platform and joined Jake and Speaker Norris. Jake handed the deed of transfer to Norris. Norris held up the deed and said, "Mr. Hearn is Director General of the Nature Conservancy and the deed I hold in my hand transfers to the Conservancy a conservation restriction to forgo and prevent future development and use of the property in order to preserve conservation values."

At first the throng of people did not seem to understand. Norris seemed puzzled.

Jake seized the microphone. "Ladies and gentlemen, this means the Cumondun family trust continues to own the property and has the ability to sell or convey the property to anyone at any time, but the Nature Conservancy will assume the responsibility for periodically monitoring the property to safeguard the conservation values and enforce compliance with the terms of the conservation restriction. *In other words, this acreage will never be commercially developed and we will never have a bridge to America.*"

Jake waited a moment until his last sentence sunk in. Suddenly there was pandemonium. The crowds of people stood and cheered. Children screamed. The high school band struck up the National Anthem. People on all sides stood and applauded and others just simply wept. It was a marvelous thing to see.

Norris put his hand over the microphone and whispered, "You know Jake, you can be sure of one thing now. You will never get any judgeship in this state as long as I am alive."

JAKE DELLANHUNT, VINEYARD LAWYER

AUTHOR BIOGRAPHY

A.J. Cushner is a retired Boston trial attorney, magazine and newspaper columnist and a graduate of Bowdoin College and Boston University Law School. He is a deep-water sailor, aviator, alpine climber, expert trap and pistol shooter, fly-fisherman and skier. He lived in West Tisbury on the Vineyard for many years and now resides in Florida.